THE LIFE AND TIMES OF
BEAU BRUMMELL

THE LIFE AND TIMES OF BEAU BRUMMELL

by

CARLO MARIA FRANZERO

ALVIN REDMAN LIMITED

LONDON

First published in 1958 by
ALVIN REDMAN LIMITED
107 Jermyn Street, St. James's, London, S.W.1

Printed in Great Britain by
Latimer, Trend & Co., Ltd., Plymouth

CONTENTS

ILLUSTRATIONS

6

PREFACE

The only moral one can draw from history is that it is much better to invent a new fashion than a new social theory. The first may improve the appearance of men; the latter will only bring about a revolution.

For this I choose Brummell as the most famous of Englishmen. Brummell is a symbol, not a mere human being. Don't let us ask what great deeds he performed or what he did for his country, or to help the people. He did only one thing—an entirely useless thing, many people would say—he invented a new fashion.

Yet, if we consider it, was it really an entirely useless thing? Of the long history of mankind what do we really remember? The changing fashions of the peoples. Indeed, the history of the world is written in the iconography of men's fashions—their dresses, their *coiffures*, their manners and ways of life.

Brummell does not belong to the political history of England, yet he is more immortal than any politician. His place in history is, indeed, loftier and yet more difficult to assess, for it is the history of English manners and taste.

Brummell was the expression of the tendencies of his times; yet his influence transcends all times. Brummell felt beauty and elegance as a woman or an artist feels it. His celebrity was due to his elegance. Like Oscar Wilde a century later, his presence in any company was a sure guarantee that the conversation would be brilliant. With Brummell his wit went hand-in-hand with style. One

7

wonders whether dandyism charmed Brummell rather on the intellectual side than on the actual side; and although he spent his life in company, he was in fact an aloof man, with an aristocratic reserve, full of impertinent disdain, ever at war with his environment. He was the man of the world in the complete sense.

Brummell's life should be purged of the trivial and unpleasant details which burden the usual biographies. He was, one may say, a vain man, and the world is pitiless towards vanity. Why? Moralists decry it with big words, even those who do not hide how large a place it occupies in their souls. Brummell was also an upstart; but he was a genius, and gave his style and his manners to the society that was by birth his superior—he gave the whole world a definition of dressing well, and he had that rare faculty of classifying at a glance the members of a company; he had a social perspective, that enabled him to approach all things and all men, and when he chose to approach them at all, in his unique manner, holding them in the palm of his hand, he added to them a new lustre and an elegance all his own.

Never has England been in greater need of a new Brummell! Brummell would have saved our world from that sheer vulgarity which is called Democracy.

I have, indeed, written this life of Beau Brummell as a counterpoise to a surfeit of Democracy. When the shabby coat with leathern patches at the elbows and borders at the cuffs came to be worn as a kind of political badge, English elegance was laid in the grave for ever, and I felt that England should have done something for the man who invented the starched cravat, an event that was, in itself, devoid of social results, but left nevertheless an impact upon the social history of England as great and immortal as the advent of the Welfare State.

As a token of gratitude for the many happy years I have lived in England may I, therefore, make my bow to Beau Brummell—an Englishman whose name will always be remembered with pleasure.

C.M.F.

I would rather be Brummell than Napoleon.

LORD BYRON

PART ONE

The Valet's Grandson

I

One rainy day in the year 1837, in the Brittany town of Caen, some urchins loitering about the street saw an elderly gentleman tottering along, keeping close to the houses. He looked like the caricature of a fashionable man, with his boots very much down at heel, trousers that had seen better days, a greatcoat with its moth-eaten fur collar turned up against the wind and the rain, and a tall hat, oh! so very shabby and yet absurdly worn at a rakish angle. The elderly gentleman was traversing the muddy cobbles with a funny step that, had those urchins only known it, used to be described as that gentleman's elegant way of walking *entre une goutte de pluie et l'autre*, between one raindrop and another. . . .

Suddenly the elderly gentleman slipped on the mud, lost his balance and fell. To the very young it is a comical sight to see an elderly gentleman in a top hat slipping over the muddy cobbles and falling with both legs in the air, endeavouring to keep his tall hat upon his wig. The urchins laughed and cried: "*Voila Monsieur Brummell, qui s'en est allé les jambes en l'air!*"

Some passers-by helped Monsieur George Brummell to get up and charitably escorted him as far as his hotel. He was certainly not in a fit condition to proceed as far as Madame de St. Ursain's for a social visit. Besides, he was bleeding and bruised, and a waiter at the hotel discovered that one of his boots was only half pulled on.

Monsieur George Brummell refused to be put to bed; he wanted to sit in his arm-chair, which was much *déla-*

15

brée, very much in need of re-upholstering. But it was the arm-chair that had been given to him by Her Royal Highness the Duchess of York. And to sit in that arm-chair, in front of the fireplace, although the grate was empty, was to enjoy once again the flow of happy memories.

Those memories! Oh, if only he had accepted the offer of the London booksellers and written them down in a great big volume! But the Duchess of York had made him promise—it seemed now so long ago—that he would never put down on paper anything connected with the Royal Family. And what was his own life but the mirror of all the follies and all the vanity that was called his friendship and his quarrel with the Prince Regent, later King George the Fourth?

The Regent—poor Prinny, so angry because he had called him fat! The memory of it brought the flicker of a smile to Monsieur Brummell's thin lips. His eyes glanced at the mantel—no, the famous snuff-box had gone long ago, even his last and very modest silver one had gone, and all his seals, his chains, his gold repeater-watch, for which he had once paid eighty guineas, all had been sold for a song. Nothing, nothing whatever remained; only his memories, and the ghosts. The ghosts he saw in this very room.

It was a tragedy to have lived too long: he was now a king in exile who had outlived his reign.

In that shabby, fireless room, Monsieur George Brummell, ci-devant Prince of Fashion and now a wreck of a man and a little mad, thought that the greatest joke of his life was that he, who had been the equal of the Prince Regent, was descended from a valet.

II

Yes, Grandfather William Brummell had been a valet. The family tree went no farther than the year 1734, when a young man of twenty-five called William Brummell had been engaged as valet by Charles Monson of Broxbourne and Spring Gardens, Vauxhall, who in that very year had exercised the Monson's prerogative of standing for Lincoln, and was returned as Member of Parliament.

William was a gentleman's gentleman of rare qualities; a valet who loved his calling as an art, and remained in the service of the Monsons all his life. He was also a man of thrift, and having married and begot two sons, whom he called William and Benjamin, he acquired with his savings a house in Bury Street, St. James, and arranged with his wife Jane the letting of the upper floors. The neighbourhood was quite fashionable, and gentlemen in town to attend Parliament or the rich young men of rank much preferred private apartments run by former butlers and valets to the rather haphazard inns.

One evening Mr. Charles Jenkinson, who was to become the first Lord Liverpool, knocked at the lodging-house in Bury Street, attracted, he used to recount, by the penmanship of the small notice in the window, "Apartments to Let". The notice had been written by the young Bill Brummell. William Charles Jenkinson, son of Charles Jenkinson of Barford Lawn Lodge in the Forest of Whichwood in Oxfordshire, who had commanded the Royal Horse Guards Blue at the Battle of Dettingen, took an apartment in William Brummell's lodging-house in Bury Street, and later on took an interest in the young man who had written the notice. Later, in 1763, George Grenville, Chancellor of the Exchequer, chose Jenkinson, now leader of the "King's Friends" in the Commons, as Joint-Secretary to the Treasury and Jenkinson found William Brummell, Jr., a clerkship in that office and made him his Confidential Secretary. William Brummell continued as private secretary at the Treasury when Lord North became Prime Minister in 1770, and was with him during the twelve years of his administration. He must have been an exceptional secretary, for Lord North conferred upon him a series of lucrative appointments: Receiver of the Duties on uninhabited houses in London and Middlesex, Comptroller of the Hawkers' and Pedlars' Office, Agent and Paymaster of the Pensioners of Chelsea Hospital, all sinecures the net salaries of which amounted to £2,500 per annum: Lord North was called by the pamphleteers "the God of Emoluments", and his private secretary enjoyed a handsome share of the good things.

After Lord North's resignation, William Brummell retired to the country and lived a life "distinguished by private virtues" at his handsome seat, The Grove, near Donnington Castle, a place famous for having been the residence of Chaucer. It is said that the enriched William Brummell "excelled for his exertions on behalf of the infant poor". It is also recorded that he was most hospitable to his affluent friends and the guests received at The Grove included Charles James Fox and Richard Brinsley Sheridan.

William the Elder had died on the last day of the month in 1770, in which Lord North was named Prime Minister. The final retirement to Bury Street had not been a change for the better; but the first Brummell recorded by history died much comforted by the thought that his son, now secretary to the Prime Minister of England, need never be a valet.

Bill, now the head of the house of Brummell, between picking up the perquisites that came his way in Lord North's office, picked up a pretty wife in Miss Richardson, daughter of the Keeper of the Lottery Office, one of the prettiest girls of her day, slender and graceful with delicately modelled features, and a mass of lovely hair such as one sees in Gainsborough's "Perdita". Bill Brummell himself was not a specimen of handsome manliness, with his long nose and long underlip; but he was a shrewd man, and the marriage with Miss Richardson was a good lottery ticket.

In 1793, Bill Brummell was left a widower, and exactly one year and a day after his wife's burial he was himself carried to the family vault at St. Martin's-in-the-Fields. He left three children, born at short intervals: Maria, William, and George Bryan, who was born on June 7th 1778, when his father was still living in London, and was baptized at St. Margaret's, Westminster, on the 2nd of July.

III

At the age of eight George was sent to Eton, the good Lord North having given to his excellent secretary nominations for both his sons, William and George. Their father was anxious to secure, by his boy's connection with Eton, a better approach to society; and through Lord North's good offices Brummell major and Brummell minor were accepted for the First Form, in which very few boys at Eton began. William was placed seventh in the list of ten and George was ninth.

Young Brummell showed no particular inclination to studies, nor did he leave his name carved in the old panelling. Neither was he fond of sports and athletic exercises. One of his school-fellows recorded George Brummell as clever but very idle, and most frank. It is added that, as a fag, he could toast bread and cheese in an unsurpassable way. But all have recorded that he was most fastidious and neat in his dress, so much so that the boys nicknamed him Buck Brummell.

The school uniform was unbecoming: a blue coat with a double row of large brass buttons, the top one of which was left open to show a bit of white waistcoat and a ruffled shirt. The cravat, also white, was tied in a bow: was there something in his nature that made young Brummell think that a cravat was an important thing in a man's personality? He took at once to wearing the wings of his cravat not only longer than it was customary but more neatly tied, overlapping the lapels of his coat.

He also had a most unusual mouth for a boy of his

age. It was small, but with thick lips which he compressed, and that gave him an air of impudence.

That air of impudence was to remain on his face for ever as the imprint of the gods.

He was also remembered for his manner and ready wit. Considering that the sons of the aristocracy lived at Eton under almost appalling conditions of accommodation and food, with a minimum of comfort, with beds of thin flock mattresses and that they had to saw logs, scrub tables and clean knives and fetch coal, one must conclude that the fastidiousness of dress and deportment—and foremost that frankness of speech and biting wit that were to become the greatest charm and asset of his career—must have come to young Brummell from the famous wits and Bucks, the term Dandy had not yet come into vogue, whom he had, as a mere lad, so often seen at Donnington round his father's table—Charles Fox and Richard Sheridan. Fox was thirty years older than little Brummell. In the years he used to visit Donnington Hall he affected a style of neglect in his dress, but there still was around Fox the aura of the days when he had sported a three-cornered hat upon a huge wig, *talons rouges* on his shoes and had posed as a leader of the fashionable "macaronis" at Brooks's Club. Moreover, the boy Brummell had heard Fox talk of the urgency of the Regency question when it could be no longer denied that George III was insane; and the boy was duly impressed by the knowledge that this man of fashion, a rake and a politician, was the mentor and idol of the young Prince of Wales. And it was from the lips of Charles James Fox that young Brummell heard the news of the French Revolution, "the greatest event that ever happened in the world and how much the best!" The greatest certainly it was; as for being the best, the opinion of Fox did appear somewhat rash to George Brummell in later years. And, anyway, political events and changes did not leave a deep impression upon young Brummell's mind—he was one of the fortunate few for whom life is a personal matter, entirely distinct from the affairs of states and peoples which are the concern of kings and politicians.

At Eton young Brummell discovered one very important thing—that his manners and his wit made him a leader among his fellows.

In the year before his father died, 1793, an event occurred to the boy Brummell that was to have an immense, an almost fatal, influence on his life—he met the Prince of Wales. [The wreck in the mean room in the hotel at Caen stirred in his arm-chair.]

Brummell used to say in later years: "My first encounter with the Prince of Wales was bucolic"; and the thick underlip pressed forward more impudently, for there was nothing pastoral in the fat prince nor in the sophisticated Beau Brummell.

Yet, the gods of the future Petronius Arbiter of that delightful period which was the Regency had ordained that his first meeting with the prince, who was to be his infatuated patron and friend and eventually his bitter enemy, should take place in surrounds that were truly bucolic.

There used to be in the Green Park a small pond. The Green Park and the little St. James's Park existed already before the Restoration of Charles II in 1660. Like the Champs-Elysées in Paris, they were for long time fields and pasture. In the time of Brummell, the small pond in the Green Park[1] was surrounded by lovely trees, which cast their pleasant shade over the walk that was called the Queen's Promenade. Not far from this pond, and not

[1] It was closed in 1856.

far from the present Clarges Street, there used to be a
rustic house blending with the surrounding countryside:
a tiny farm, a stable where a few cows were kept, with
rambling roses everywhere. The place belonged to an
aged lady-farmer, a Mrs. Searle, who continued to live
there till 1815, always walking about in an old-fashioned
dress and a tall bonnet, swaying with grace in a gown
à paniers. During the American Wars George III had entrusted Mrs. Searle with looking after the small place,
and the Princess Marie, the fifth child of George III's
fifteen children, had herself decorated the rooms. This
royal patronage had made Mrs. Searle *à la mode*, and the
maids-of-honour and ladies-in-waiting of the Queen used
to visit the charming cottage after their duties at St.
James's Palace, which had then a right wing, balancing
the still existing left one, till it was destroyed by fire in
1809.

One day in 1793 the Prince of Wales and the Marchioness of Salisbury crossed the Green Park and entered
Mrs. Searle's farm-yard. Her ladyship pulled up her
skirts and went to help, or at least to watch, Mrs. Searle
milking her cows, while the Prince of Wales remained in
the yard chatting affably with a striking and pleasant
young lad of about fifteen years of age. "This is my
nephew, George Bryan Brummell, Your Highness,"
called Mrs. Searle from the stable. "He has just finished
his schooling at Eton, and this very year he will go to
Oxford. A very good boy is my nephew George, and
clever too."

The Prince glanced amiably at the young man: surely
he looked pleasant and handsome too. Perhaps, thought
the Prince, what was most pleasing was his air of good
grace and the assurance of his manner; there was a kind
of respectfulness mixed with audacity—or was it just that

worldly air that Eton so peculiarly bestows? The young Prince of Wales—he was at the time thirty-one—asked affably: "What would you like to be when you leave college?" Young Brummell looked at the tall and well-built Prince of Wales, graceful of manner, although already inclined to portliness; he took in with a look of careful and envious appraisal the *recherché* attire of the Prince, the white curly wig, the immaculate and snowy buckskin trousers, the highly glazed boots *à l'écuyère*, the well-cut habit buttoned high, the large cravat of perfectly laundered lawn out of which emerged with some difficulty a double chin. Then he replied: "I would like to be an officer in the Army." The Prince looked down on the boy, and smiled at the conceit: "Well, young George Brummell, come to see me again when you come down from Oxford, and I will give you a Commission in my regiment, the 10th Hussars."

The Marchioness of Salisbury had returned from her bucolic enjoyment with Mrs. Searle, and the Prince and the lady returned to their carriage. Young George Brummell stared after the Prince: he had already seen him some days before at Windsor, *caracolant* in all his glory amid his brilliant officers, as Colonel of his regiment; and he had also seen him in his equipage, with the coachmen and lackeys in green liveries, coming out of Carlton House. It was a marvellous expectation to look forward to, the patronage of the glittering Prince of Wales.

IV

After the summer vacation of 1793 George Brummell went to Oxford, entering at Oriel.

He did not burn midnight oil over his books: he consumed a considerable quantity of midnight oil, but in more congenial occupations. In fact, one feels inclined to think that he wrote for the Newdigate Prize as a joke: when he missed the prize, his friends said that his failure was mainly due to his indolence in having neglected to scan his lines. Yet his copy was considered the second best!

Oxford was a place for social training rather than a preparation for scholarship. One could—or might—acquire a taste for learning; Charles Fox had acquired it, and Brummell picked up—but just picked up—that taste of reading for the sake of reading that he preserved all his life and which gave to his quick mind that veneer of being knowledgeable which is, at all times, so much more attractive in a gentleman than the weight of erudition.

At Oxford young Brummell read, wrote occasional stanzas as fashion demanded, ordered his horse at hall-time, turned a tame jackdaw, with a pair of bands on, into the quadrangle to parody the Master, and systematically violated all college rules.

But he progressed in the exclusive habits to which he had shown himself so inclined at Eton; and discarding the little that remained of schoolboy frankness, he followed his inclination to be the paragon of correctness.

He was not yet sixteen, and there must have been a

good deal of *naïveté* in this young *poseur*, so anxious to appear a Prince of Lordliness. But he was a born leader of fashions, and his little affectations of speech and manner were greatly admired. It was, most of all, his natural wit that fascinated and conquered his fellows: from the day when, at Eton, he had saved the very life of a poor bargee by saying to the boys who wanted to throw the fellow into the river: "Don't do that, in the state of perspiration the poor fellow is he will most certainly catch a cold!"

At Oxford, Brummell developed those characteristics for which he became famous—aplomb, fastidious neatness of dress and a quick and witty repartee. Was he also vain? Vanity is the strongest incentive to glory. And Brummell came into the world with an inordinate love of glory and a great admiration of the unusual. He acquired that disdain that in future years made him look at the world with his chin in the air; that mien of superior majesty that even gave a twinge to the Prince; that contempt for necessities that made Bulwer Lytton put in his mouth: "Though starving at school, I never took twice of pudding, and paid sixpence a week out of my shilling to have my shoes blacked."

The career of George Brummell was decided in those Oxford days: he would go for the great world and would be a star in that world. To this intent he chose his friends with care and discarded them with ruthlessness. If they were high-born, he was endowed with brighter gifts; if they had rank or money, he had the prestige of his manners and the flair for saying the right thing at the right moment. Society and rank would be the background for his natural talents.

His father's death was the determining factor in George Brummell's life. There is an element of fatality in the life of the chosen of the gods. William Brummell had died in March 1794. He died as a gentleman at his country seat of Donnington, was buried in St. Martin's-in-the-Fields —and left a gentleman's will, with reasonable bequests to charity. The bulk of his fortune—some £65,000—he left to his three children, to be theirs at their coming-of-age.

George Brummell lost no time: his inheritance, though, for the time being only the income therefrom, offered him an unhoped for opportunity. He shook the dust of academic studies off his boots, and decided that he would enlist in a crack regiment and invest his guineas in the thousand per cent of fashionable life.

He went to London, a mere lad of sixteen, but full of determination, and so handsome, and the mirror of correctness. Fortune always favours the audacious. Indeed, he carried Fortune's crest in his pocket, engraved as a seal upon a little burnt topaz at the end of a pocket-pencil: a tiny ship in full sail, with the waves below, and around the top the Latin motto *Fortuna iuvat*.

One day he was brought again to the Prince's presence. Did the Prince remember the promise he had made to the boy at Mrs. Searle's farmhouse, one year before?

In 1794 young Brummell had all the qualities which most appealed to the extravagant Prince of Wales; he was good looking, and the Prince adored beauty in man or woman; his speech was attractive, he had a ready tongue and an aplomb that was almost amazing in one so young. He charmed the Prince. He repeated, with the utmost good grace, that the thing he desired most was to beg the Prince to permit him to enter his regiment "and be near *him* all the time". It was impudent and so naïve!

In a moment of good humour, the Prince nodded a promise; perhaps he would like to see more of this handsome and entertaining young man—so many others at Carlton House were dull!

On the 17th June 1794 George Brummell was gazetted to a cornetcy in the 10th Hussars, the Prince's own regiment.

V

Brummell did not particularly seek a soldier's life, but life in the 10th gave him all the opportunities for the life he wanted. Dressed—one would almost say adorned—in the rich uniform of the Hussars, which suited his slight and handsome figure to perfection, Brummell found himself at once in the highest society, in a position that he had never dreamed of attaining. The attractiveness of his character and the perfection of his manners helped to promote friendships and intimacies with his brother officers, and the 10th Hussars was the regiment of the sons of dukes and earls: there was Lord Edward Somerset, son of the Duke of Beaufort; Lords Charles and Robert Manners, sons of the Duke of Rutland; Lord Charles Kerr, son of the Duke of Roxburgh; young Bligh, son of the Earl of Darnley, and young Lumley, son of the Earl of Scarborough.

The grandson of William Brummell, the valet, entered this grand world serenely. A far from negligible factor was the marked patronage of the Prince. The Prince of Wales was then thirty-two, a handsome young man, in the stiff and lymphatic way of the House of Hanover: and he was at the height of his follies. Out of all the dullness and commonplace of George III, narrow, bigoted and insane, had come a brood of dissolute children: the Prince of Wales was the embodiment of the most violent reaction to the paternal traits. His debts amounted already to £640,000; and for nine years the Prince had been "secretly" married to Mrs. Fitzherbert, a liaison that was all the worse because the beautiful widow was a Roman Catholic. Compared with this, his previous infatuation for Mary Ann Robinson, the lovely "Perdita" of Drury Lane, had been no more than a silly boy's mischief, although George III and Queen Charlotte would have willingly paid five thousand pounds for their son's letters to the Irish actress. Perhaps the fault rested, as it is often the case in many families, with George III, who, as a father, was a queer man: honest, impeccable, but very obstinate, a man who had boasted to his unruly sons that he had never had a weakness, and could not permit it in anyone else. George III had nine sons: the Prince of Wales, the Duke of York, the Duke of Clarence (who was to succeed the Prince of Wales as William IV), the Duke of Kent, father of Queen Victoria, the Duke of Cumberland, the Duke of Sussex, the Duke of Cambridge. It was a good thing that the counties of England offered a fine choice of titles for such a brood of royal dukes. There were two other sons, Octavius and Alfred, but they had died very young. There were also six daughters: Charlotte Augusta, married to King Frederick of Wurthemberg; Augusta-Sophia; Elizabeth, married to the Landgrave of Hesse-Hombourg; Mary, married to the Duke of Gloucester; Sophia and Amelia.

George III's Prussian system of education had produced nothing but detestable results in his children: nearly all his sons and daughters had chosen to make clandestine marriages. But the one who most worried the King was the Prince of Wales.

It is true that his adventure with Mrs. Fitzherbert was a mere incident in his amorous career, for his love affairs went on till the end of his life; and whenever he found an obstacle he lost his head and profited by his grieved appearance: he had the habit of blood-letting by his physician so as to appear pale and wan before the lady of his heart!

Maria-Anne Fitzherbert had been a clever woman. Having sent to the grave in twelve months her first husband, Edward Weld, and disposed of Mr. Fitzherbert with the same speed, Mrs. Fitzherbert at twenty-six was in all the splendour of her beauty and very popular in society. She commenced by spurning all the advances made by the Prince and, to be on the safe side, went to live in Lorraine. The Prince bombarded her with letters, and at last she returned. Then the Prince became dramatic, and gashed himself in the chest. He did not die but he bled like an ox, and the lovely widow, more frightened than moved, ran away again. Upon this His Royal Highness spent his days at Mrs. Armstead's, the mistress of Charles Fox, howling like a dog to the moon, beating his head, pulling his hair, rolling on the ground, threatening to renounce the throne, sell his plate and jewels and emigrate to America with the woman he loved. At last, Mrs. Fitzherbert came back, and soon afterwards her secret marriage to the Prince of Wales was the talk of London.

One year later, in July 1786, the Prince had set out for Brighton, accompanied by his morganatic bride and a trunkload of economical resolutions. The Prince went to stay at a house in the Steine, which had been leased, *pro forma*, by his confidential clerk of the kitchen and general factotum, Louis Weltje, and released to his royal master at a rent of £150 a year, an underhand transaction that saved inconveniences to the Prince who was up to the topmost fold of his neckerchief in debts. Mrs. Fitzherbert was settled in a villa close by, and remained there until, several years later, the architect William Porden built for her the house which still exists on the Steine.

In the meantime the Prince made his clerk of the kitchen Weltje buy the property originally leased, and without delay commenced building the "Marine Pavilion" which was, in later years, to become the fantastic residence that still stands today, an incredible confectionery of Indian domes and cupolas outside, charmingly decorated inside in the style that used to be described as Chinoiserie. The first building, however, designed by Henry Holland, the architect of the Drury Lane Theatre, was of simple classical design, consisting of a central rotunda, with wings to north and south, each with large bow-windows on both the ground and first floors and elegant ironwork balconies. That original building still forms the core of the present pavilion: the *salon*, as it was called from the beginning, was already circular as it is in the later building, and crowned by a shallow dome surrounded outside by classical statues on Ionic columns. The dining-room was in a wing so close to the kitchen that the guests used to say that it was "a steaming dinner". The Prince's bedroom was over the breakfast-room; it was hung with quilted chintz, and the bed hangings were of silk, chequered green and white. A famous feature of the apartment was "a broad window, so situated as to afford the Prince an extensive view of the sea and Steine as he lies in bed". There was also another feature, not reported in the chronicles, and it was a secret tunnel through which Mrs. Fitzherbert could reach the Prince's bedroom from her own house. Later, Mrs. Fitzherbert had a new house built in the grounds, with four different cellars: a small beer cellar, an ale cellar, a wine in casks cellar and a wine in bottles cellar. And there were many and vast cellars in the pavilion as well. It was a house of deep potations.

For the already mentioned reason of debts, the Marine

Pavilion was purportedly built by Weltje, who leased it to his royal master for twenty-one years at a yearly rent of one thousand pounds. At this house the Prince spent the summer and part of the winter, occupying his time in hunting, racing, and entertaining his friends, in rooms which, to be in keeping with his Asiatic Pavilion, he kept at tropical temperature with an immense stove. After the fall of the Bastille, in 1789, hundreds of refugees of the French Revolution had arrived in Brighton, which was at the time one of the chief cross-Channel ports, and many of those noble *émigrés* were received and entertained at the Pavilion.

It was at the Marine Pavilion that young Brummell was properly initiated to the vagaries and eccentricities of his royal patron and of his gay Court.

It was a queer sort of Court. Unpopular in London, where his romantic ardours, his perpetual life of disorders, his theatrical poses were considered too much even by the fashionable set, the Prince found Brighton a more congenial residence in which to let himself go and follow in the steps of his dissolute uncle, the Duke of Cumberland, who, to spite his brother the King, had decided with his wife to debauch the heir to the throne; in this they were helped by the example of the Duc de Chartres, later Philippe Égalité, who before the Revolution, used to cross the Channel quite often. The Court at the Marine Pavilion was a strange medley of brilliant officers, politicians, dancing-masters and pugilists. In fact, no better was Carlton House in London: Angelo, the fencer, Jack Radford the stud-groom, Davidson the tailor and Weltje the clerk of the kitchen were in town the confidants and paramours of His Royal Highness. No better, in a sense, were Fox or Sheridan. Charles James Fox, the most gifted of men and the most admired, at twenty-one had been acclaimed head of a great party and a Prince of Eloquence but he had not waited to be of age to be in debt to the extent of an astronomical sum. He was capable of remaining at a gaming-table for sixty hours without rest, sleeping and eating on the very table of pharos, and when he was cleaned out he even borrowed from the footman of his club. And Richard Brinsley Sheridan, the fortunate author of *The Duenna*, *The School for Scandal*, *The Critic* and *The Rivals*, was such a gambler and so burdened with debts that his house in Saville Row had to be guarded by his servants against intruders. With his nose the colour of royal purple, Sheridan had installed himself at Carlton House and visited occasionally the Pavilion at Brighton, to be welcomed as "Sherry". And there were plenty of ladies, and they were not too particular.

Each night the Prince's table was a symposium of the usual *habitués*, a sprinkling of political orators and a posse of little arrogant scribblers, and eccentric men of the world such as the Duke of Norfolk, who was all his life a great friend of Fox. One could meet him at night in the most ambiguous places, sometimes dressed as a clergyman, sometimes as a jockey. He was also a great bibber, and in *The Times* of February 1794 one reads: "The Duke of Norfolk has had an attack of rabies; he cannot stand the sight of water. His doctors have prescribed him to look only at wine. The Marquis of Bath and Lord Thurlow, who were present at the consultation, have decided to follow the same diet."

There was the Marquis of Queensberry, old and worn out, who in town used to pass his time looking through his quizzing-glass at the beauties in the park. And there was Lord Onslow, alias Tom Tandem, proud of his new *attelage*, and driving all day through the city in his black phaeton with four black horses; and there was Lord

Barrymore who dressed in livery the bailiffs that were in possession in his house. And there were Francis Rowdon, first Marquis of Hastings, later Lord Moira, future Governor of Bengal, and the pleasant Lord Cholmondeley, a man full of anecdotes, and Lord Coleraine, who was the black soul of the Prince.

At that time the fashion was to go on the Continent to acquire a finish and *la politesse*: French taste and French manners. Many of the London gentlemen had known the Court of Versailles and the *délices* of the Petit-Trianon, the promenade on the terrace, the concerts in the Orangerie, the magnificence of Fontainebleau and the hunt at Saint Hubert and Choisy. They knew Lauzun, Richelieu, Boufflers, the Comte d'Artois, and they tried to live up to their morals. The Prince did not know Paris, but he pretended to know all French high society, and used to mention their names in the most inopportune way.

In this strange milieu, a Court where gravity and ceremonial went hand-in-hand with vulgarity and drollery, young Brummell found it easy to progress; indeed, he realized that it would be within his grasp to become the leader.

VI

As for regimental duties, Brummell did little or none. He was so much with the Prince that he was seldom present with the corps, to the extent that he did not know his own troops: all he knew was that one of his men in the front rank had a very large blue nose, that was for Brummell a beacon. One day this man was transferred to another troop, when Brummell was seen to arrive, late as usual, and finding the regiment already in line he rode up and down looking for the man with the blue nose; until at length he stopped opposite the nose. "How now, Mr. Brummell!" bawled the Colonel. "You are with the wrong troop." "No, no," muttered Brummell, looking at the blue nose. "I know better than that; a pretty thing indeed if I did not know my own troop!"

His air of gentle impudence, his wit and refinement disarmed everyone. One night at a ball given by a great Law Lord in Russell Square, a Miss J, a great beauty who afterwards became Lady G.H., refused all invitations to dance, till, late in the evening, Cornet Brummell was announced: he made his bow to her, and the lady, who had probably been waiting for him, rose from her chair and giving her hand to the brilliant officer, was soon figuring among the crowd of dancers. Later in the evening, Brummell asked a friend who might be the ugly man near the chimney-piece. "Surely", answered the friend, "you know the master of the house!" Quickly came the reply: "No, how should I? I was never invited."

One day he drove into the barrack-yard in his carriage,

with four post-horses. "Hallo, George," called a brother officer from the messroom window, "when did you take to four horses?" "Only since my valet gave me notice for making him travel with a pair."

Army life at Brighton was a gay farandole. Events of the war across the Channel were celebrated with a *feu-de-joie* and great dinners with the Prince at the Pavilion or at the Castle Tavern. The Prince did all he could to ingratiate himself with the Brighton folk: gave them concerts with his own band of musicians, and once he had a marvellous tent put up at great cost, and in this tent he entertained his friends in martial style. Mrs. Fitzherbert used to enliven military parades by attending in her phaeton, sometimes on horseback, dressed in the Prince's uniform. Most of the officers were accompanied by their ladies, either official or unofficial wives. The most fashionable courtesan of the day, Harriette Wilson, was often in residence at Brighton under the protection of the young Marquis of Worcester. Generals and high foreign officers would ride down from London, inspect the Prince's regiment and spend a gay night at the Pavilion. The Prince enjoyed these visits immensely; the *Public Advertiser* recorded that his principal amusement was in manœuvring his regiment.

In April of 1795 the regiment was told that they were needed at the end of the month for a very important occasion. The Prince was to be married to the Princess Caroline of Brunswick. A party of the regiment, commanded by Lord Edward Somerset, escorted the Princess from Greenwich to St. James's Palace.

At the august ceremony, on April 8th, Cornet Brummell was in personal attendance upon the Prince as *chevalier d'honneur*, and after the wedding he went down with the royal pair to Windsor. He gave a description of the honeymoon that was in strong contrast with the one given by the Princess herself in her *Diary illustrative of the times of George the Fourth*.

One feels inclined to believe Brummell. He went, the morning after the wedding, to take the Prince's orders while His Royal Highness was at his dressing-table and the impression he received from the conversation with the Prince was a most favourable one: "The young couple appeared perfectly happy and satisfied with each other, particularly the Princess, who was then a very handsome and desirable-looking woman."

According to other sources the Princess Caroline was a sort of good-hearted but crude young woman, brought up in one of the smaller German Courts, and far from suited to the tastes of her bridegroom or of his entourage. Lord Malmesbury had been sent to her father's Court to escort her to England, and he confessed to friends that he had not been able during the journey to persuade her to wash adequately or to change her underclothes frequently enough. And Princess Caroline loved badinage in the wrong places. The match was doomed from the start.

However, from Windsor Brummell accompanied the Prince and his bride to Brighton for the summer. His collection of songs and stories served him well—he played with grace and ease the Boccaccio to the Prince's Court.

Nine months after the royal wedding, on 7th January 1796, a child was born, Princess Charlotte. But Caroline was frivolous, the Prince was fickle; they bored each other.

At the end of April the Prince wrote to Caroline that neither should be held answerable to the other because nature had not made them suitable to each other. He wanted peace; he proposed that their intercourse be restricted to tranquil and comfortable society. The Princess complied.

VII

What was it that made Brummell soon tire of military life? Some *beaux esprits* said he wanted to emancipate his head from hair-powder which was still worn in the army, while it had been gradually falling into disuse in society, since Pitt had laid a tax upon it three years before. Lord William Murray, a son of the Duke of Atholl, had taken out a patent in 1796, for making white powder from horse-chestnuts so as to evade Pitt's impost on powder made from flour; but the Duke of Bedford and his friends had pledged themselves to forfeit a sum of money if any of them wore their hair tied and powdered, and in September of 1795 a general cropping and washing and combing out of hair took place at Woburn Abbey in the very room which for so long had been dedicated to powder-puffs.

Others said that Brummell, in 1798, was not at all anxious to seek "a reputation at the cannon's mouth" for the cause of suffering humanity in that disturbed state of Europe.

Maybe there was no reason at all. Late one evening in the early part of 1798 the news reached Brighton that the 10ths were to be transferred to Manchester. Early next morning Captain Brummell—for the Prince's patronage had enabled him to progress rapidly and be promoted to the rank of Captain on the 1st June 1796—made his way to the Prince, who expressed some surprise that his friend Brummell should pay him a visit at such an early hour. "The fact is, Your Royal Highness, I have heard that we

39

are ordered to Manchester. Now you must be aware how disagreeable this would be to me. I could really not go: think, Your Royal Highness, Manchester! Besides, you would not be there. I have, therefore, with Your Royal Highness's permission, determined to sell out." It was all very tactful, and with such a touch of romantic flattery. "Oh, by all means, Brummell, do as you please."

So ended George Brummell's career in the most dashing regiment in the Army. And he was not yet of age, barely twenty years old.

The human wreck in the dejected hotel room remembered it quite well. The house at No. 4 Chesterfield Street had very soon become a rendezvous of the fashionable *élite*. In the sitting-room on the ground floor one could find, towards midday, the most elegant men of London, envying the privileged ones who were allowed upstairs, to contemplate the Beau completing his toilet. Now and then Robinson the valet would come downstairs carrying over his left arm a score of cravats: "Our failures," he would say, smiling, and disappear through the pantry.

Sometimes the Prince of Wales would arrive and talk with his friend or ask his opinion about a new coat. Often the discussions would extend until the hour of dinner, when the Prince would condescend to remain. More than once the Beau reduced the Prince to despair by a sarcastic comment on his clothes. Once the Prince began to blubber when told that Brummell did not like the cut of his coat!

Then the Beau would sail out, to his club or for a stroll in Bond Street as far as St. James's, invariably dressed in a blue coat, a buff-coloured waistcoat, and either lace boots or light pumps. His trousers were black, closely fitting and buttoned above the ankle. His charming bearing and perfect figure were his chief attractions.

He was not particularly handsome: he was fair, almost red-haired, with a lofty brow, a thin sharp nose which he carried much in the air, his lips slightly compressed, his clear eyes of an indefinable shade—a little quizzing with a strange expression of disdain and alert irony; but he was about the height of Apollo and the proportions of his body were perfect, whilst his hands were particularly well shaped, "he could indeed have found an engagement to perambulate France from fair to fair to personate the statuary of the ancients"—but he was incomparably distinguished from head to foot.

In two years George Brummell had become the leader of London fashions. How had he done it? The choice of residence had been most apt: it was opposite the apartment occupied for a time by the witty George Selwyn, one of the *élite* of fashion whose fame Brummell had soon caused to wane. In fact, the settling in London was the determining decision of his life—it set him on the threshold of history.

The year he had left the army career, he had come into possession of his estate. Quite modest, barely some £30,000, perhaps not equal to his position: many of his noble friends had income many times his modest capital.

But the splendour of George Brummell was intellectual, and his power was his intelligence.

He had purchased a few good horses; had provided himself with a good cook; in his rooms he gave some excellent dinners at which guests were as carefully chosen as the wines, and like his companions he was fond of "deep drinking", seeking the emotions to be found in the emptied glass; but even with one foot in the chasm of inebriation he could remain the master of his wit and of his elegance. There was in him something that attracted and captivated the attention of a great epoch, an achievement which is not attained merely by the graceful wearing of splendid clothes. Indeed, Brummell attached much less interest than has been supposed to the art of dressing; much less than many other men. His tailors were Schweitzer and Davidson, of Cork Street, who were also tailors to the Prince, and a German tailor named Meyer who had his shop in Conduit Street, but they were not fathers of his fame. Brummell scorned to share his fame with his tailors; he considered it much better to trust alone in the nameless grace of polished ease, which he possessed to a remarkable degree.

From the outset he ruled by his perfection of dress and manners: it was at that time that he coined the great axiom of the man of fashion: "To be really elegant you must not be noticed."

History came to call him the Prince of Dandyism; but the term Dandy suggests vulgarity: a "dandy" used to be a taproom measure, and in Johnson's Dictionary the nearest approach to the word is the dandelion, certainly a vulgar flower. Moreover, in the matter of dress the Dandies were given to extravagances, such as excessive padding, trousers containing cloth enough for a whole suit, collars sawing off the wearer's ears with the corners threatening to put out the eyes, wrist-bands intruding upon his plate, and a hundred other eccentricities, like the Green Man of Brighton who, a few years later, walked out every day dressed in green from head to foot, green suit, green shoes, green gloves, green handkerchief, green hat, till one fine day the Green Man jumped from his window.

When Brummell came upon the London scene at the

end of the eighteenth century, men's dress had become exceedingly slovenly. A few years previously, refinement of dress had been an actual mania, the followers of this cult being called Macaronis, a name first given to those who had done the Grand Tour and visited Naples: young Charles Fox devoted himself passionately to the Macaronic cult, wearing a huge wig with a tiny three-cornered silk hat absurdly poised upon it, and shoes with red heels and the rest of his dress as the caricatures of the period depict him.

But later on Fox and his friends affected a style of neglect, throwing a sort of discredit on proper attire. This neglect spread from the House of Commons to the clubs of St. James's and to all society. In 1794, with the triumphant era of Jacobinism and Equality in France, men's dress in London seemed to be perishing. The formal dress with knee breeches and buckled shoes, which till then was worn by all gentlemen and persons of note, became confined to Court levees and drawing-rooms, and gentlemen took to wearing pantaloons, cropped hair and shoe-strings; buckles and ruffles almost disappeared, together with the hair-powder. Even the ladies, having cast off their tresses, now exhibited heads *à la victime* and *à la guillotine*. Only on the pavements of Bond Street did the Macaronis make a great display of their enormous wigs tied up behind and their coloured stockings, while the *Muscadins*, notwithstanding the general horror of all that came from France, had adopted the latest Paris fashion, with the very long tail coat, the tail of hair, and the wide stock surrounding the chin with waves of muslin—a fashion reminiscent of the *Incroyables*. Bond Street, built in 1686 under Sir Thomas Bond of Peckham, Controller of the Household of the Queen Mother, was now the fashionable promenade of all London; Laurence Sterne lived in Bond Street on the first story of No. 41, Sir Thomas Lawrence lived at No. 24, Lord Byron always put up at Stevens's Hotel, No. 18; one could see Lord Sandwich's—that inveterate gambler who invented "the sandwich" so that he could go on with his gambling without stopping to eat—and Fox's chairs and Walpole's carriage, or Sheridan crossing from his house in Saville Row and going to Brooke's.

The Prince of Wales had, since his youth, assumed the position of leader of fashion, but the results were far from satisfactory. The Prince's first attempt in fashion was to wear a new kind of shoe buckle, which he had invented, a magnificent affair, really quite new, and of which he was very proud, for this buckle which was only one inch wide, was five inches broad, reaching almost to the ground on either side of the shoe. At the first Court ball the Prince attended he dazzled all the company with the splendour of his dress: a coat of pink silk-damask with white cuffs, a waistcoat of white satin embroidered with white foil and adorned with a profusion of French paste; and his hat was ornamented with two rows of steel beads, with a button and loop of steel and cocked in a new military style. When he had taken his seat in the House of Lords, the Prince had worn black velvet, embroidered with gold and pink spangles and lined with pink satin; his shoes had pink heels and his hair was much pressed at the sides and fully frizzed, with two smart curls at the bottom. Even now, at the age of thirty-three, he had not learned restraint in dress, and at a great ball at Brighton he appeared in a velvet suit of a dark colour with green stripes, superbly embroidered down the front and seams with a wide embroidery of silver flowers mingled with foil stones; the waistcoat was of white and silver tissue embroidered like the coat; the garter ribbon was fastened with a shoulder-knot of diamonds, and on his chest glittered a profusion of Stars and Orders.

Also for outdoor or ordinary wear the Prince loved a luxurious wardrobe. In fact, he spent a fortune in dress. Often a plain coat, after repeated alterations by Davidson the tailor, who journeyed to and from London and Windsor, would cost £300 before it actually met with the Prince's approval. In his lifetime he assembled an immense array of coats and vests and breeches and topcoats, and kept them in his wardrobe year after year, a vast and incredible collection of clothes of which he was enormously proud, and on which he had spent a fantastic sum. After his death they were sold for barely £15,000.

Some of the Prince's friends copied his splendour, but by 1790 Charles Fox had discarded the fopperies, the long curls, the spying-glass, the red heels and his bouquet that was nearly large enough for a maypole: now Fox wore the blue frock-coat and the buff waistcoat that were to become the uniform of the Whigs, and Fox often wore them till they were threadbare. Yet the Whigs had the patronage of the Prince, and Fox, who lodged in St. James's Street, held a levee of his followers and of the members of the Gambling Room at Brooke's. Rarely purified by ablutions and wrapped in a fouled nightgown open to reveal his hairy chest, with his hair dishevelled, he dictated his politics which the heir to the throne imbibed with gusto.

The advent of George Brummell in London had changed all this slovenliness of dress. Backed by the Prince, Brummell laid down the law.

The first follower, or disciple, of Brummell was the Prince himself. The Prince was vain, extremely vain of what he considered his exceptional good looks, and per-

haps he found the new style set out by Brummell particularly becoming to himself. For although he showed a great
love for music and played the 'cello "better than any
prince in Europe" and was quite proud of playing with
Rossini (whom he used to put out of tempo), and liked
singing and painting, his strongest inclination was for
dress. He was, indeed, portrayed in every costume and
every imaginable dress, with powdered wig and without
it, with or without a tail, with wigs fair, brown or black,
dressed as a Hussar, a Dragoon, a Field Marshal, or in
the knee-breeches and stockings of black silk with the
Garter above his knee.

Brummell chose a course middle-way between the extravagance of the Prince himself and the utter neglect
prompted by the eccentricities of Fox. And Brummell's
success was achieved by the poise he possessed in a
unique way. Maybe his poise was a pose, and Brummell
knew the full value of pose, that pose and poise which,
combined with a touch of impudence, impressed the
world to the full. He created his own legend, and imposed it upon the world. Probably not one-tenth of that
legend was true; but it was believed as gospel, and it still
survives today.

VIII

It was said that Brummell lived for the art of dressing. It was said that every day he spent long hours in his dressing-room; that his morning toilet was a most elaborate affair; that he was never guilty of *déshabillé*; that he treated his dressing as a cult or a profession and, like a true man of business, he devoted the best and earliest hours of his day to his toilet. His dressing-room was like an artist's studio, in which he daily prepared that elaborate portrait of George Brummell which was to be exhibited for a few hours in the clubrooms and the *salons*, only to be taken to pieces again and again created in a different style for the evening. The *batterie de toilette* was of fine silver and included a spitting-dish, for its owner "could not spit into clay".

It is to this early period of Brummell's reign that belong the incredible and often fantastic stories: that his gloves were made by two different men, one for the thumbs and the other for the fingers and the rest of the hand; that it took him a couple of hours to wash; that after shaving he plucked out all superfluous hair with a pair of tweezers and a dentist's mirror. One day a young man, who was fascinated by the gloss of his boots begged Brummell to give him the recipe he used for blacking— "Blacking, my dear sir? Well, you know, I never use anything but the froth of champagne." And to another who asked him the address of his hairdresser: "I have three: the first is responsible for my temples, the second for the front and the third for the occiput." As Madame de Staël said: "*Quand il s'agit de Brummell la manière dont il coupait ses ongles est importante : l'âme se mêle à tout!*"

Yet, the secret of Brummell's elegance was simplicity and cleanliness. "No scents," he used to say, "but plenty of fresh linen and country bleached." He made a point of boasting that he changed his shirt three times a day, and that he sent his linen to be laundered in the country, for the country air and sun bleached it and gave it a unique fragrance!

It indeed required plenty of linen and fragrantly fresh to perform the miracle of the famous cravat that he invented. The neckcloth, or stock as it was also called, was then a huge cumbrous wrap, worn without stiffening of any kind, clinging to the neck and bagging in front. In a moment of inspiration Brummell decided to have his muslin starched. It took infinite pains, hours and days of patient toil to reach the miracle of this perfect cravat: but it was a stroke of genius.

The method by which the result was attained has been recorded by his faithful disciples: "The collar, which was always fixed to the shirt, was so large that, before being folded down, it completely hid his head and face, and the white neckcloth was at least a foot in height. The first *coup d'archet* was made with the shirt collar, which he folded down to its proper size; and then, standing before the looking-glass, with his chin poked up towards the ceiling, by the gentle and gradual declension of his lower jaw he creased the cravat to reasonable dimensions, the form of each succeeding crease being perfected by using the shirt which he had just discarded."

It was an entertaining sight to see Brummell performing this delicate transient masterpiece. Quickly and deftly he would wind the cravat round his neck and tie the knot, pull the collar down over the cravat, and slowly lowering his chin he would crease the cravat to the proper height by the most simple and natural method in the world. Performed in the twinkling of an eye, the result must be successful at the first attempt or not at all. The least misjudgment in the pressure of the chin would spoil the effect, and another fresh cravat would have to be inserted again and tied. Yards and yards of starched muslin were tied and discarded each day. As Robinson the valet said: "Our failures."

The success of the cravat in London was tremendous. The first time Brummell appeared with his starched neckcloth it created a sensation. Nothing else was talked of for days in fashionable circles. In the clubs, members courted George Brummell for the grace and favour of a lesson in tying the new cravat. But no one ever succeeded in reaching Brummell's perfection. The secret of the pressure of the chin and the final touches with the hands covered by the discarded shirt was never revealed. Indeed, some went to such exaggeration in the matter of stiffness that the cravat might have been laughed out of court had not Brummell himself delivered a devastating rebuke. One night, at Brooke's, he asked the footman: "Is Lord Worcester here?" The nobleman was seated next but one to Brummell, but his face was almost lost in the mounting creases of his super-starched cravat. "Yes, sir," replied the waiter. After a pause Brummell said: "Is his lordship ready?" "Yes, sir." "Then tell him that I drink his health," and raised his glass without turning his head.

The cravat became the object of caricatures and lampoons. One anonymous author wrote a satirical brochure entitled *Neckclothiana*, in which all the possible and impossible variations of the cravat were described: the Oriental Tie (*couleur de la cuisse d'une Nymphe ennuiée*), the Mathematical Tie, the Osbaldiston Tie, the American

Tie (the best colour is Ocean Green), the Napoleon Tie, the Mail Coach Tie, the Trone d'Amour Tie (*couleur yeux de jeune fille en extase*), the Irish Tie, the Ballroom Tie (*blanc d'innocence virginale*), the Horse-collar Tie, the Hunting Tie (*couleur Isabelle*), and the Maharatta Tie (*couleur peau d'Ispahan*).

No perfumes, had said Brummell; and in a period when baths were not common and gentlemen recoursed to distilled eau-de-roses to cover their lack of morning ablutions, George Brummell said: no perfumes but plenty of fresh linen and country washing.

Lord Byron once described Brummell to Leigh Hunt as having nothing remarkable in his style of dress except a certain exquisite propriety. Cleanliness was the touchstone with which Brummell's acquaintances were invariably tried; to detect in them any variation from that virtue, which he placed higher than godliness, was enough to make him decline any further intercourse with them. One day one of his friends asked him how he had passed a day with a certain family and what sort of people they were: "Don't ask me, my dear fellow," replied Brummell; "I actually found a cobweb in my night-pot. . . ." It was probably after this experience that Brummell took to keeping a travelling one, in a folding mahogany case, with a carpet bag for the same. He objected to country gentlemen being admitted to his club, because their boots stank of horse-dung and bad blacking. It was his passionate love of cleanliness that made him object to the prevailing devotion to stables, dog kennels and coachmanship.

His morning dress was similar to that of every gentleman—Hessian boots and pantaloons, or topboots and buckskins, with a blue coat and a light or buff-coloured waistcoat; of course fitting to perfection. In the evening

he wore a blue coat and white waistcoat and black pantaloons: the trousers which opened at the bottom of the leg
and were, after being put on, closed tightly by buttons
and loops, were suggested by Brummell to his tailor
Meyer: Brummell was the first to wear them and they
immediately became the fashion. With these trousers he
wore, for the evening, striped silk stockings and carried an
opera hat. His sedan-chair was always brought to the
foot of his staircase, and from there he was carried immaculate to the hall of the house he deigned to visit.

Brummell's good taste was gospel to his tailors: to a
nobleman who went to Schweitzer and Davidson to be
properly rigged out and asked the tailors what cloth they
would recommend. "Why, sir," said old Davidson, "the
Prince wears superfine, and Mr. Brummell the Bath coating. Suppose, Sir John, we say Bath coating. I think Mr.
Brummell has a trifle the preference."

Nothing was too trivial for Brummell to achieve the
perfect result. As he could not induce his valet to polish
properly the edge of his boots, where the sole met the
uppers, he took brush and blacking and himself gave a
demonstration of how it should be done, and finally
issued instruction that the soles of the boots must be
polished as well as the uppers. A minute speck upon the
white of his neckcloth or shirt was enough to send it back
to the washerwoman.

He never wore anything extravagant, no white satin
and dove-colour. Brummell disposed for ever of those who
mistake eccentricity for elegance: "If John Bull turns to
look after you, you are not well dressed, but either too
stiff, too tight, or too fashionable." He was the quietest,
plainest and most unpretending dresser. It was the total
absence of all peculiarity and a rigid adherence to the
strictest rules of propriety in costume which gained for

51

him the homage due to his undisputed taste. He eschewed colours, trinkets and gewgaws. His clothes were exquisitely made and, above all, adapted to his person. He put them on well, too: but for all this there was no striving for effect; there was an unusual absence of show in his appearance.

The simplicity of Brummell's dress, like simplicity in writing, was only achieved with great artifice. It was a case of the perfect art which conceals art; that effect of spontaneity which can be achieved only by taking infinite pains. The style he affected misled many men into thinking that they had only to copy him to achieve the same effect; they did not know that the distinction of his dress was part of the distinction of Brummell himself, his own and inimitable.

The days when a man of quality was recognizable by his dress had ended with the French Revolution. It was Brummell's genius to reveal to men that a man in plain clothes could walk as a king.

IX

For England it was an epoch of great wars on the seas and on the Continent, and of profound social rumblings inside the country; and yet, it was also a time of unequalled frivolities.

At the end of 1792 the French had already begun hostilities by laying an embargo on all British shipping in French ports, and in February 1793 England had retaliated by acting in the same manner, although there were more British ships in French ports than French ships in English ports.

In February, after the message of King George III to Parliament, war was actually declared—a war that was to last twenty-two years. The Duke of York, Colonel of the Guards, was made General, and he addressed the regiments and told them that he would accompany them to Holland. The war was to last until after Waterloo; unpopular and yet stubbornly fought, like all British wars in history. King George III was ill. The King's illness was described for many years as "the most painful event", painful in more than one way, for the King was mad and the Prince of Wales was, many people thought, no saner than the King: the Bill to make the Prince a Regent went, for years, in and out of Parliament. It was, indeed, the issue of the two great contending parties and leaders: Fox and Pitt. Luckily, now and then the physicians reported that the King was "recovering from his malady".

The Revolution in France still continued, and London saw the *émigrés* arriving in increasing numbers, till in 1794 it was found that the British Fleet had brought off from Toulon 14,877 men, women and children. No wonder that Parliament voted the Alien Act!

The *émigrés* brought in Parisian fashions, which at that time were particularly fantastic; and the French Revolution, although being fought as the enemy, sent in the Rights of Man. The news of the victories by Lord Howe and Lord Nelson were duly celebrated; but the misadventures of the troops in Holland were not equally popular. Never was there an epoch when the lampoonist and cartoonist were more unbridled. The attire of men and the Prince's Court appeared too much of a carnival.

Brightelmstone—as Brighton was still called—was the place where the fashionable youth congregated, so much that the new fashions were called Brighton dress. The extravagant clothes ranged from tight lacing to the scaramouch; there flourished those curious specimens which were nicknamed the Macaronis, a home-made macaroni being called a "Jessamy"—the Jessamies being the equivalent of the Victorian "mashers", harmless and rather effeminate, entirely taken up with the contemplation of their external appearance. The cocked hat went out, and the "chimney pot" was inaugurated: alas, at its inception it was limp, made of felt; but it soon gained strength and lustre, and although today more rarely seen and smelling of camphor it still shines.

The Jessamies became the Beaux, a name that soon gave way to the Dandies. And the "chimney pot" was worn *au naturel*, without trace of wig; and the swathed cravat succeeded the more refined jabot. But for great functions, such as the King's drawing-rooms, men still bedecked themselves in great finery: embroidered silk and silk velvets; we read of a Mr. Skeffington who, for the King's birthday of 1794, wore a brown spotted silk coat

and breeches, with a white silk waistcoat richly embroidered with silver, stones and a shade of silk, the design
being large baskets of silver and stones, filled with bou-
quets of roses, jonquils, etcetera, the ensemble producing
a beautiful and splendid effect; and of the Marquis of
Lorn wearing a blue and brown striped silk coat and
breeches with a white silk waistcoat embroidered with
dentelle and shades of silk; and of Lord Willoughby de
Broke in a dark-olive spotted silk coat and breeches, with
a white silk waistcoat, and the suit richly embroidered in
blood-coloured stones and many shades of silk.

Mention of hair-powder appears in *The Times* of
November 1794 (although it may be a libel) that "as a
Frenchman cannot exist without a powdered head, and
meal being so dear in France, the Beaux are under the
necessity of wearing *powdered whiting*. Rouge is plenty
enough; the ladies therefore, as usual, wear their faces
under red masks." All this was completed by the Prince's
Bow which every man of fashion strained to copy; and no
other style of bowing was ever more ludicrous.

Ladies' fashions also were tried at Brighton; and a
series of prints were published recording the amount of
indebtedness ladies owed to Art, to repair the ravages of
Nature. Waists disappeared, and high feathers came in as
adornments of the head, with such a grotesque *panache*
that the lampoonists wrote that at all elegant assemblies
the lustres and chandeliers were removed and the doors
carried up to the height of the ceilings: for a matter of
expediency, ladies' feathers were generally carried in the
sword-case at the back of the carriage! High heels became
the rage, and towards the end of the century, the fashion
of "nudity" was such that "the most elegant fig-leaves
would be all the rage". Again *The Times* was writing, in
December 1799: "The fashion of false bottoms has at least

this utility, that it compels our fashionable fair to wear something."

It was at Carlton House and at the house of the Duchess of Devonshire that Brummell came into contact with the most famous of his contemporaries.

Like the Prince of Wales, the Duchess Georgiana of Devonshire made her house a literary and political *salon*. From her childhood Lady Georgiana Spencer had held promise of being unusually intellectual as well as beautiful; and her sensible and excellent mother (a daughter of Stephen Poyntz) bestowed the greatest care and exercised the greatest judgment on the cultivation of every attainment that could improve her daughter's mind and figure. Her success complete; Georgiana was elegant in mind and body, although the pietists and moralists might detect in her a deficiency in strength of character and dignity, for she was enthusiastic but volatile. Maybe rank, wealth and beauty had a somewhat ruinous effect; yet, when she married the Duke of Devonshire, in 1774, Georgiana Duchess of Devonshire soon appeared as the true model of the fashionable woman of the eighteenth century, and the eighteenth century lasted much longer in England than in France; it extended, in England, into the nineteenth, both in dress and manners and divisions of society in classes and castes.

At her marriage, Georgiana Duchess of Devonshire was only seventeen years of age—at that time aristocratic perspective husbands had a preference for "sweet seventeen" —and placed by an indulgent husband in possession of the means to gratify all her whims. Soon she became the authority on every idle fashion; her name was attached to every novelty in dress, and even the colour of her carriage was known, for several years after her death, as the

"Devonshire brown". She introduced Nelson's or Egyptian hats; she translated Petrarch, studied the lyre, dedicated her poetical attempts to the Abbé Delille—that Abbé Delille who went into exile in 1795, and after a stay at Basle came to London, where he translated *Paradise Lost*. Her beauty and brilliancy attracted a host of admirers and flatterers—Charles James Fox, Wyndham, Burke, Sheridan, Lord Townshend, Fitzpatrick, and many others, who formed her court in that Devonshire House in Piccadilly, whose huge wrought-iron gates gave to the large town-house a delightful country-house appearance, and to all who still remember it make painfully regretful its disappearance. The fame of the Duchess Georgiana of Devonshire rests on her attainments and errors rather than on her beauty; she was one of those women whose success derives from their charms. That she was beautiful of face and body was admitted by all, for her hair, tinged with red, and her face reminded one of that other beautiful woman from whom Georgiana Spencer descended, Sara Jennings, wife of John Churchill, first Duke of Marlborough; but her fascination lay in the grace of her deportment, her irresistible manners, the seduction of her society.

Politics were in the fashion, and like the Prince of Wales who professed Whiggism to induce Parliament to pay his enormous debts, the Duchess's *salon* was a Whig Club; but Georgiana was an honest partisan. It has remained a by-word in the history of English political elections the part played by the Duchess of Devonshire in Fox's election, when, in 1784, he began his struggle with Pitt, and the Duchess Georgiana put a cockade in her hat and a scarf of the colours of her candidate across her breast, and went in her carriage to do the round of his constituency, with Lady Duncannon and the Duchess of Rutland, entering cottages and shops, until the day when she purchased the vote of a butcher with a kiss.

When the American War broke out, the Duchess Georgiana was at Tiptree and Warley Camps dressed in the uniform of the Derby Militia, an example that roused a military fever amongst the women, which was followed by a naval enthusiasm after the victories of Howe, Duncan and Nelson; and her Aboukir and Nelson bonnets and head-dresses were all the fashion. On the declaration of war against France, the Duchess set to work with her friends to knit flannel waistcoats for the troops exactly as it happens in our days!

There were bouts of gaming in the Duchess's life, for she was devoted to faro, the fashionable game of the day; a passion that brought her into situations greatly detrimental to her character and to the dignity of her high station; and in the short space of three years after her marriage, her extravagance made her the butt of public criticism in many pamphlets: the motto of one was: "Pleased with a feather, tickled with a straw"; yet, between vagaries and errors she founded at Devonshire House the coterie of "All the Talents". Fox was the leading spirit, probably helped on this favour by his devotion to gambling. To those years belong the episode of the evening when Fox came skipping into his wife's drawing-room in South Street, and went capering round the room chanting: "Great run, great run! *Vingt-et-un*; lucky dog; tomorrow morning pay the Jews, pay them all!" Unfortunately for him, and for them too, it was Friday night, and on the Saturday night all the cash that Fox had won was carried again in bags to his club and there lost again down to the last sovereign.

Gibbon was one of the Duchess's admirers; in a letter he wrote eloquently in her praise: "You are much too

young to have known Georgiana Duchess of Devonshire,
and therefore felt *la belle passion* for her, as every man did
in my day."

But Georgiana was a poet of no mean wing; her translation of Petrarch's thirty-fourth sonnet is a remarkable
example of her sound knowledge of the Italian language:

> *Levommi il mio pensier in parte, ov'era*
> *Quella, ch'io cerco e non ritrovo in terra.*

> *In spirit I had mounted to the sphere*
> *Where she amidst its gentle inmates beam'd,*
> *whom still I fondly seek, but find not here*

is creditable for any poet and translator.

The cleverness of Brummell consisted in this, that he
was not a man of extravagance in life, any more than he
was in his dress. He was well aware that he was a person
of comparatively small means; he had, therefore, elected
to live in an elegant but not expensive way.

His house in the Chesterfield Street was furnished and
decorated in the manner suitable to a gentleman, and
Brummell set right away a taste for Buhl furniture and
Sèvres porcelain, a preference which he retained all his
life. On the walls there were portraits of Admiral Nelson,
Lord North, the Duke of Rutland and the heroes of the
day. In his small library were prominent the *Letters of
Lord Chesterfield*, the *Memoirs of the Chevalier de Grammont*
and the volumes of the *Edinburgh Review*. Later, on his
occasional tables he began to assemble his notable collection of snuff-boxes of great value and beauty. He also had
a beautiful collection of canes. He did not keep a carriage
for town use, and used a sedan-chair to avoid the mud.
Only years afterwards he used a carriage in town. He was
not fond of hunting, but made it a point to have always

first-class horses for his use in the country, in the best conditions, and relied upon a dealer named Fryatt who bought horses for him.

Life in London centred round the clubs and the drawing-rooms, and the summit of social life was the privileged circle of the Prince's friends at Carlton House. The first thing Brummell did after settling in London was to become a member of White's.

At the beginning of his career he was generally with the Prince or with his friends at Brighton, and seldom visited the London clubs. But in London it became natural and advisable to join one or more of the right clubs. At the end of the eighteenth century a gentleman joined a club as part of his existence. The membership was not only well guarded but reserved to the gentlemen who had a definite position in society; in fact, the total membership of the clubs at the time amounted to no more than some twelve hundred. A small world, in which everyone knew each other and there were no trespassers, for they were all of the same family and class, almost a caste, what the Viennese aristocracy so aptly called *hof-fähig*, the people of the Palace. A fashionable man walked in Bond Street and St. James's, and spent many hours at his club. There were no sports in London, although Lord Byron was fond of mixing with pugilists; golf was yet confined to Scotland; a man of fashion, when in town, had little to do except to pay calls, go to receptions or balls and visit his club. The club was also a place to have a meal, as there were no restaurants at all. And at his club a gentleman could do as he pleased, sit down to dinner in morning dress or, if it pleased him, in his nightdress.

In resigning his commission in the 10th Hussars Brummell was elected a member of White's. In 1799 he was elected also at Brooks's: there is an entry in the Memorials of Brooks's—"Mr. Brummell, proposer and seconder Mr. Fawkener, date of election 2nd April 1799."

Brooks's was founded by a Mr. Brooks, a wine-merchant and money-lender who had taken over the older and famous Almack's Club, which had been established at No. 5 in Pall Mall opposite Marlborough House in 1764 by a Scotsman, William McCall by name, who however called himself Almack. The idea of such a venture occurred to McCall when he saw the success of Mrs. Cornely's at Carlisle House in Soho Square. Almack had chosen his site well, obtaining leases of various properties to the east of Pall Mall Place; he commissioned Robert Mylne to design a suite of assembly rooms, which actually were in King Street and were later known as Willis Rooms; and in February in 1765 the new premises were opened under the patronage of a royal duke. There were twenty-seven original members, including the Duke of Portland, the Duke of Roxburgh, the Earl of Strathmore and Charles James Fox; and the rules of the club were certainly quite original, for they decreed that no gaming should take place in the eating-room on penalty of paying the whole bill of the members present; that dinner shall be served up punctually at half-past four o'clock in the afternoon and the bill be brought in at seven; and that any member becoming a candidate for any other club (old White's excepted) should *ipso facto* have his name struck out of the book.

Almack's became, at a later period, merely an assembly for dancing; but originally it was, like all other clubs, a place for gaming. Yet, Almack's remained to the end a place of selectness, a club which blackballed with a freedom and a capriciousness that made people say that one could hardly conceive the importance which was attached to getting admission to Almack's, the seventh heaven of the fashionable world. Draconic laws were imposed by the patronesses, for Almack's was also a ladies' club, and once the Duke of Wellington was turned from the portals of Almack's because he was wearing trousers and not knee-breeches, which had been made indispensable by the Committee sitting in conclave.

In 1778 Brooks moved to premises on the west side of St. James's Street, and formed a new club to which he gave, as it was customary, his own name. It started with one hundred and fifty members at the modest subscription of four guineas; in 1791 the number had increased to four hundred and fifty. Brooks's was considered a Whig Club, as was also White's; but Brooks's was more in the run, for Charles James Fox, who lived nearby, made a habit of having his supper-parties catered and wined by Brooks's; and Mr. Brooks often hastened to the rescue of a member in financial straits; a generosity that was quite in contrast with his acumen as a money-lender, and at his death in 1782 he was in poor circumstances. The greatest patron of Brooks's was perhaps Fox, who used the club as his house and made it a seat for his debating society, at which he would plan his parliamentary campaign. In a letter of George Selwyn to Lord Carlisle of 21st March 1782, one reads: "I stayed at Brooks's this morning till between two or three, and then Charles Fox was giving audiences in every corner of the room and that idiot Lord Derby telling aloud whom he should turn out, how civil he intended to be to the Prince, and how rude to the King."

Also the Prince of Wales was a member of Brooks's, but later he resigned as a protest against the blackballing of two of his intimates.

White's derived its name from White's Chocolate House, which had existed since 1698, five doors on the west side of St. James's Street coming up from the Palace.

In 1733 the house had been destroyed by fire, and the Chocolate House was removed a few doors higher up: the fire at White's is recorded in one of Hogarth's plates of a "Rake's Progress" representing a room at White's where the gamblers are so interested in their gaming that they do not hear the alarm given by the watchmen who are bursting open the door.

The Chocolate House had become a private club soon after it was founded, and in 1736 it numbered amongst its members the Duke of Devonshire and the Earl of Chesterfield; and in 1745 it was so popular that a second club was established and called the Young Club to distinguish it from the Old Club. In 1755 White's, Old and Young, moved to No. 38 St. James's Street.

There were other clubs: Byron mentions in a letter that he belonged to the Alfred, the Cocoa Tree, the Union, the Watier (which, however, was not yet founded at the time when Brummell settled in London), the Racket's (which was at Brighton), the Pugilistic, the Owls, and several others; and there was Boodle's originally called the Savoir Faire when it was founded in 1762 at 28 St. James's Street.

All these clubs were famous for the furious gambling; many old families still suffer from the passion for cards that had taken hold of their forebears in the Regency years; it was said of Crockfords that family fortunes literally ran on the four aces. But in those early years Brummell did not gamble; he was too busy conquering his kingdom in society.

The period that went from the end of the eighteenth to the first twenty years of the nineteenth century was a living thing; it has become almost legendary. It was also a time of transition, wedged between the two centuries. The old order of life still survived and the new order, which found its culmination after Napoleon's fall, was enwrapped into a cloak of romanticism that gave colour and richness of touch also to the fast-moving changes in politics and social evolution. There was, as it should be, a "decorative class" of citizens; never the expression "Upper Ten Thousand" had more accuracy of meaning. Happy were the times when a gentleman could look at the wars going on in Europe and on the seas without feeling any democratic qualms! "Bony" and the war against France was a matter for Parliament and the Admiralty, as it should be. "Life" had its centre at Carlton House, and at the Prince's Court the war against Napoleon was not of paramount interest.

Carlton House had been built exactly facing the present Waterloo Place in 1709, by Henry Boyle Baron Carleton, descendant of the Carleton who had been artistic buyer for Charles I for his collection of pictures. From the Carleton family Carlton House had come into the hands of the royal family in 1732, and was the residence of the Princess of Wales, mother of George III. In 1783 it became the official residence of George III's eldest son, the Prince of Wales, who restored it extensively at an enormous cost, decorating it with a collection of armours of every age and every country, including the famous swords of Bayard the Knight *sans peur et sans reproche*, of the Duke of Marlborough, of Louis XIV and of Charles II. He also added to the armours a collection of Flemish pictures, and a collection of men and women who were certainly not specimens of virtuous living.

George Brummell became the favourite at Carlton House for three reasons. The first one was that he possessed the qualities most esteemed by the Prince among things human, youth, and the youth of George Brummell was set off by the assurance of a man with experience and able to dominate circumstances. The second one was his bold and most delicate mixture of impertinence and respect. The third one—and probably the one that played the most important part upon such a superficial and vain man as the Prince, all taken up by concern about his personal appearance—was the genius of dress.

Carlton House was the summit of London's social life; and at Carlton House George Brummell acted as the model, guide and mentor to the Prince of Wales.

X

In the briefest of time Brummell was the undisputed King of Society. How did he do it?

He did not reach the summit by his money, for compared with some of his friends he was a poor man. He did not reach it through the Prince's protection and patronage, for the Prince of Wales was free and easy with his friendship and intimacy with many gentlemen of his entourage, and equally easy he was in dropping them at the slightest displeasure.

George Brummell became the leader of fashions and the absolute dictator of London society by his genius. There are men who are born to rule: George Brummell was born to rule over the fashions of his times. And he ruled by his good taste in dressing and manners, and by his wit and impudence.

It was not merely because he dressed well that he became the leader of society. On the other hand, Brummell understood instinctively the importance and the influence of dress upon society. In this respect he was an innovator; he established for men the modern form of dressing almost as we know it today. At a time when men still dressed in gay colours and there still lingered the knee-breeches and the silk and velvet coats that until the French Revolution had been the typical dress of a class, Brummell launched and imposed the trousers, which he devised with his German tailor. The prevailing spirit of revolutionarism may have helped the spreading of this innovation; but while Pitt in 1802 could still be seen in

66

the streets of Cambridge wearing the cocked-hat of earlier days, and Charles James Fox also affected the older style, and Lord Erskine in the same year was breakfasting in a dark green coat and scarlet waistcoat and silk breeches, and the Prince of Wales constantly appeared in public wearing garments of striped green velvet embroidered with silver flowers and a powdered wig adorned with a profusion of curls, George Brummell was already changing the dress of gentlemen to the uniformity of trousers and a coat which was sober of colour and cloth and relied for its effect solely on the cut and on the distinction of its wearer.

But Brummell scorned to share his fame with his tailor and to give his name to cloaks and hats. He had the "nameless grace of polished ease" that set him high above other men. His entrée to the finest houses in the land was never disputed; his friendship was considered a privilege by the bearers of the proudest names—and in this Brummell was certainly helped by his intimacy with the Prince and by his few years in the finest regiment.

Perhaps in Lister's novel, *Granby*, there is the truest and shrewdest characterization of George Brummell. He had great powers of entertainment, a keen turn for satire; he seldom committed himself by praise or recommendation but left his example to work its way; and could talk down his superiors with cool confidence. He saw the advantage of being formidable; he sensed gullibility and without affecting short-sightedness, he could assume that calm but wandering gaze which veers, as if unconsciously, round the prescribed individual, neither fixing nor to be fixed, a look which perhaps excuses you to the person you cut, and, at any rate, prevents him from accosting you. He had both wit and impudence. Impudence is not rudeness: it is the utmost detachment of the genius who feels himself above all other men. Impudence can manifest itself in witticisms, or be epigrammatic. Impudence in life is what an epigram is to a book or a play—the leaven of dialogue and conversation. George Brummell's disdain for lesser men expressed itself in supercilious witticism: less than a century later the last of the dandies, Oscar Wilde, expressed the same disdain in epigrams, but the approach of these two geniuses to life and manners was the same.

The history of Brummell is, indeed, written upon sayings, often absurd, like that of Byron who said that he would rather be Brummell than Napoleon. The real meaning of such a saying is lost; perhaps Byron meant that Brummell's empire of taste and fashions was more imaginative than Napoleon's empire of countries and peoples.

Brummell was a mass of contradictions: he could be exquisitely polite and appallingly rude; he could say telling things or be as gay as a young boy. The clubs resounded with laughter when Lord Alvanley recounted the story of how, that afternoon, the Prince of Wales, who had just received the present of a horse, asked Brummell for his opinion. Brummell instead of examining the animal in the usual way, went behind the horse and studied its tail for a considerable time, till the Prince at last asked him what he was doing. "Sir," Brummell answered, "you should never look a gift horse in the mouth."

The ladies were anxious to have him at their balls and parties; more than one hostess spent anxious hours awaiting the arrival of Brummell, who would at long last enter the room: lingering for a short while on the threshold, he would look round through his spy-glass, then exchange a few compliments right and left, and depart for another ball, in his sedan-chair. Brummell disliked coaches and carriages, considered the *vis-à-vis* the most inconvenient of conveyances because the steps folded inwardly, and always used his sedan, which was lined in white satin, all quilted, with down squabs on the seat, and it had a soft white sheepskin rug.

His sarcasms were generally launched at the parvenus who forced themselves into notice. With his superiors, or his equals, he was merely witty. When Pitt inquired what could be done to forward his interests, Brummell simply requested the Prime Minister to bow to him in public.

Even Madame de Staël, when she visited London, was haunted by a dread of his disapprobation, and considered her failure to please him as the greatest *malheur* that she experienced during her residence—the next was that the Prince of Wales did not call upon her! It seems, however, that Brummell had played upon Mme de Staël the joke of pretending that his great friend the most indebted Lord Alvanley was immensely wealthy and a most excellent prospective husband for her daughter Albertine—Libertine as Brummell had nicknamed her, though the girl, Byron assures us, was perfectly all right.

The businessmen who resided in the City were, as far as Brummell was concerned, living in an unknown land. One day when a great merchant requested the honour of his company at dinner at his home in the City, Brummell replied: "With pleasure, if you will promise faithfully not to tell anyone." And to an ex-Secretary of the Admiralty, who possessed great political and literary talents, but who had taken residence in the district of Bloomsbury, when invited to dine in that region Brummell piquantly inquired where he was to change horses.

He also could give an agreeable effect to words that could be very pointed. There was a gentleman in London who, in his youth, had very beautiful hair, naturally frizzy, and it was his habit to take the air in the park accompanied in his curricle by his pretty French poodle. One day Brummell, who was on horseback, met the man and the dog driving together, and he hailed the gentleman: "Ah, my friend, how do you do? A family vehicle I see!" In fact, the gentleman, quite well known in the world, was called by the sobriquet of Mr. Poodle.

At an Ascot meeting Brummell walked his horse up to the carriage of a lady who, quite flippantly, expressed her surprise at his throwing away his time on her or running the risk of being seen talking to a very unfashionable person. "My dear lady," he replied, "pray don't mention it; there is no one near us."

One night he arrived at the club rather late, and his friends asked him: "Where did you dine tonight?" "Dine? Why with a person of the name of R——s. I believe he wishes me to notice him, hence the dinner; but to give him his due, he had begged me to make up the party myself, and I asked Alvanley, Mills, Pierrepoint, Mildmay and a few others, and I assure you that the affair turned out quite unique. There was every delicacy in or out of season. But, my dear fellows, conceive my astonishment when Mr. R——s had the nerve to sit down and dine with us!"

One day a friend met him limping in Bond Street and asked him what was the matter. Brummell replied that he had hurt his leg, "and the worst of it is that it is my favourite leg". Having been asked by a sympathizing friend how he happened to get a cold, his reply was: "I left my carriage yesterday evening on my way to town from the Pavilion, and the infidel of a landlord put me into a room with a damp stranger!" To an acquaintance who asked him, during a very unseasonable summer, if he had ever seen such a one, he replied: "Yes, last winter."

The limit of his impertinence was contained in the reply he gave when he was asked what sort of a place was a certain country seat where he had fancied himself invited and, after one night, had been politely given to understand that he was in error: "It was an exceedingly good house for stopping one night in."

And his reply when asked at table if he liked vegetables: "I don't know; I have never eaten them." Then after some reflection: "No, that is not quite true; I once ate a pea."

But the most famous of his replies—so witty that Oscar Wilde pinched it in full and planted it in the first act of *The Importance of Being Ernest*—was the one he gave when someone, while assisting at his levees, asked him which lake he thought the finest in the Lake District. Brummell rang the bell for his valet: "Robinson!" "Sir!" "Which of the lakes do I admire most?" "Windermere, sir." "Ah, yes! Windermere, so it is. Thank you, Robinson." And turning to his friend: "Yes, I like Windermere best."

In the great country-houses he was a welcome guest. He was a frequent visitor of the Duke of Devonshire at Chatsworth; and rooms were always kept for him at Cheveley, the seat of the Duke of Rutland. In January 1799 he was present at the coming-of-age of the fifth Duke of Rutland, in company with the Prince of Wales, the Duke of Argyle, Lord Jersey, the Marquis of Lorne. In fact, at Belvoir he was "a friend of the family", and his rooms were as sacred as those of the Duke of York. For the coming-of-age of the Duke of Rutland, the festivities at Belvoir lasted three weeks and were conducted in a truly ducal scale: fireworks of the most splendid description were let off in front of the castle, a whole bullock was roasted on the bowling-green of the quadrangle and another at the bottom of the hill; but the weather was so cold that—so the chronicles said—"while

one side was roasting the other was freezing". Nevertheless, the peasants went in their hundreds to the Duke's
kitchen and servants' hall, and the "brown October"
was not only drunk on the premises but carried away in
pailsful.

Brummell went to skate on the ice clad in a pelisse of
fur, and one morning he was mistaken by the people for
the Prince of Wales and loudly cheered. But Brummell
was not a great skater and did not rival the Marquis of
Lorne in engraving his cipher on the ice. In fact, he hated
personal exertion in any way, and it was difficult to make
him give up a book (he was a great reader) and shoulder
a gun and join in a scramble over hedgerows and ditches.
Nor was he much of a shot. His greatest feat with a gun
was done at Cheveley: the party were contemplating the
magnificent fruits of their shooting, three hundred heads
of game; and Brummell, having accidentally caught sight
of two tame pigeons which had lovingly perched on one
of the chimneys, tempted by a standing shot, carefully
raised his gun and brought them both down. Alas, they
were the pets of one of the servants! He used to recount
it in later years: "The only time I brought down a brace
of birds it was at Cheveley, and they were tame pets. . . ."

Neither was he a great rider. Though he kept a stud
of horses, mostly for use at Belvoir, he never was a
"Melton man", and his friends were much surprised when
he joined them in the hunt, for he did not like it; it did not
suit his habits, and his servant could never get him up in
time to join the hounds if it was a distant meet, but even
if the meet was near Brummell would only ride a few
fields, and soon would pay a visit to the nearest farmhouse to satisfy his enormous appetite for bread and
cheese, and then head for home, and say that he "could
not bear to have his tops and leathers splashed by the

greasy galloping farmers". And he would lunch with the Duchess and the ladies at two o'clock and be the most sociable and amiable companion to them.

He always appeared at the covert side admirably dressed in a white cravat and white tops to his boots, a fashion that he had introduced and which superseded the brown tops; his horses were always in as high condition as their master's, and the horses were stabled at The Peacock at the bottom of the hill, near Belvoir, under the care of Fryatt, who was to Brummell more of an agent than a groom and bought without consulting his master; in fact, sometimes Fryatt put money into Brummell's pockets besides mounting him well. After a few seasons the stud was removed to Knipton, a charming village about a mile and a half from Belvoir Castle.

After he had retired from the 10th Hussars, Brummell was tempted to accept a Majority in the Belvoir Volunteers raised by the Duke of Rutland; and during one of his many visits to Belvoir, a General Officer was sent by the Horse Guards to inspect the corps: official notification of time and place was given, and General Binks from London arrived to the minute. The men were on parade; the officers were there; the drums and colour; but Major Brummell was not there. The indignant General waited and snorted and then commenced the performance of his now unpleasant duty, when, almost at the end, Major Brummell appeared in a scarlet coat coming at speed across the country, and at long last he was cap-in-hand to General Binks who addressed the delinquent officer in the manner of a real martinet: "Sir, this conduct is inexcusable; if I remember right, sir, you had once the honour of holding a Captain's commission under His Royal Highness the Prince of Wales, the Heir-Apparent himself, sir! I should be wanting in my duty, sir, if I did not, this very evening, report this disgraceful neglect of order to the Commander-in-Chief as well as the state in which you present yourself in front of your regiment. You may retire, sir!"

Brummell bowed in silence, and did retire; but after going a few paces he turned his horse, returned, and said in a subdued tone: "Excuse me, General Binks, but in my anxiety to explain this unfortunate business I forgot to deliver a personal message that the Duke of Rutland desired me to deliver when I left Belvoir this morning. It was to request the honour of your company at dinner." The General coughed and then cleared his throat to express his thanks: "Ah, really I feel, and am, much obliged to His Grace: pray, Major Brummell, tell the Duke I shall be most happy; and Major Brummell, as to this little affair, I am sure no man can regret it more than you do. Assure His Grace that I shall have great pleasure in accepting his very kind invitation." And they parted, whit broad smiles.

But Brummell had to run in all haste to the castle and prepare his friend the Duke for an unexpected visitor, General Binks, whom he had invited on the spur of the moment, not as an impostor would to get out of a difficult position, but with all the fun of a schoolboy who, on being reprimanded by his master, thinks of a sudden: "Now I will show you one!"

XI

We do not find a particular woman in Brummell's life. There were many women; many of them illustrious—the Duchess Frederika of York, the Duchess Georgiana of Devonshire; but there was never one woman who lit the fire of love and passion in George Brummell.

As he cannot be suspected of sexual inversions—at that time the secret society of homosexuals was not yet such a feature of London life—one can only say that Brummell did not love anyone but himself. The perfect dandy was a world unto himself; he could not disarrange his countenance and perfect poise by succumbing to passions or falling in love—and a man in love, as we all know, is no longer master of himself.

Brummell, a man uniting all natural and artificial attractions, stopped, as far as women were concerned, at the threshold of gallantry. It was, in him, a natural attitude. And anyone who knows women realizes that this was certain to prove his very power over them: he wounded the romantic pride of those proud ladies and set their minds dreaming.

Thus the King of Fashion had no mistress. A better dandy than the Prince of Wales, Brummell was without a Mrs. Fitzherbert; a Sultan without a handkerchief. No illusion of the heart or of the senses could modify or suspend his judgment. And a word from George Brummell was final—he was the autocrat of opinion. At the risk of being overheard in the middle of a ballroom, a Duchess (the *hauteur* permitted to this rank in London's drawing-rooms is well known even in these days) told her daughter to be careful of her manners and her replies should Mr. Brummell deign to address her; for at that first phase of his life he still mixed with the crowd of dancers at balls, where the most beautiful sat awaiting his invitation. Later on he abandoned the habit of dancing, as too commonplace for him. He used, then, to stand a few minutes at the door of a ballroom, glance round, criticize in a sentence, and disappear. He knew the value of the maxim: in society stop until you have made a good impression, then be off.

His youth, his brilliance, his charming and cruel wit, abused and adored by women, inspired many passions: but nothing transpired. Lady Jersey has been mentioned as one whom he was supposed to have taken away from the Prince. But Lady Jersey remained Brummell's loyal friend, and love affairs ending in friendship are rare. So far as we know, only one woman used words which conceal (or reveal) a disappointed passion: the courtesan Harriette Wilson; but she was probably more jealous of Brummell's fame than of his heart. "It became", she wrote in her *Memoirs*, "the fashion to court Brummell's society, which was enough to make many seek it who cared not for it, and many more wished to be well with him, through fear, for all knew him to be cold, heartless and satirical." But the courtesan Harriette Wilson belonged to those women who, in the words of Barbey d'Aurevilly, would never forgive him for being as graceful as they, and likewise many men would never forgive him for not being, themselves, as graceful as he.

Brummell was certainly once on the verge of matrimony, but, for some reasons that were never disclosed, the idea was negatived by the girl's parents. It is also said that once, though not with a lady of rank, he nearly "passed through a gold ring", for he interested the damsel sufficiently to induce her to consent to elope with him during a ball in Grosvenor Square; but a servant of the girl's mother caught them in the next street. It is said that when a friend rallied him for his lack of success in another matrimonial speculation, and pressed him for the reason for his failure, Brummell replied with a smile: "What could I do, my good fellow, but cut the connection? I discovered that Lady Mary actually ate cabbage!"

On the other hand, his honesty in love affairs was quite extraordinary. One morning at a country-house, he came into the library of his noble friend and host, and told him with much warmth that he was very sorry indeed but he must positively leave the house that morning. "Why, you were not to go till next month!" said the host. "True, true," replied Brummell anxiously, "but I must be off." "But what for?" "The fact is—I am in love with your Countess." "Well, my dear fellow, never mind that: so was I twenty years ago. Is she in love with you?" Brummell hesitated, and said faintly: "I believe she is." "Oh! That alters the case entirely," replied the Earl; "I will send for your post-horses immediately."

One woman has left us a description of Brummell as a lady's man, herself a woman of the greatest interest—Lady Stanhope. Lady Hester Stanhope was one of the most intriguing and fascinating characters of that period, which was so rich in personalities who, for freedom or for love, lived the most extraordinary lives. Brought up at her father's country seat of Chevening in Kent, at twenty-four years of age she had run away from her father's house owing to his excitable and wayward disposition; and three years later, in 1803, had taken charge of the house of her famous uncle, William Pitt. Lady Hester was a woman of beauty and talents; she possessed also considerable business acumen, and ran her uncle's affairs when Pitt was out of office. On his death she was granted a pension of £1,200 a year. She then took house in London, in Montagu Square; but her too-pointed wit made her many enemies, and in 1810 she left England for ever. After many wanderings Lady Hester settled among the Druses on Mount Lebanon, and from her lonely house of Djoun, a few miles from Sidon, dressed in the garb of a sheik, she wielded an almost absolute authority over the surrounding district, maintained by her commanding character and by the Arabs' belief that she possessed the gift of divination. The memoirs of Lady Hester Stanhope, narrated, in six lengthy volumes, by her physician Dr. Meryon, present a most lively picture of this strange woman's life and of London in the first quarter of the nineteenth century.

That Lady Stanhope was on terms of close friendship with Brummell is indicated by many episodes and references. One day, Lady Stanhope's carriage was in Bond Street, and Brummell was leaning upon the door talking with Lady Hester, whispering to her the secret of a marvellous perfume, when there walked by a young Colonel whose name was then in all mouths. "Who ever heard of his father?" murmured Brummell with his customary superciliousness. "And by the way," replied Lady Hester, "who ever heard of yours?" But Brummell's repartee was ever ready: "Ah, my dear Lady Hester, who indeed ever heard of my father, and who would have heard of me, if I had been anything but what I am? It is my folly that is the making of me. If I did not impertinently stare duchesses out of countenance and nod over my shoulder to a prince, I should be forgotten in a week; and if the world is so silly as to admire my absurdities, you and I may know better, but what does that signify?"

How true, how true! This anecdote is given in several memoirs, and it might have been merely an invention of the witty Lady Hester; but how truly it epitomized the hero of the day! There is a letter of Lady Stanhope to George Brummell, dated 30th August 1803, and bearing the Cheltenham postmark: "If you are as conceited as formerly, I shall stand accused of taking your groom, to give me an opportunity of writing to you for his character. All the inquiry I wish to make upon this subject is, to be informed whether you were as well satisfied with James Ell when you parted with him, as when he had Stiletto under his care. If so, I shall dispatch him at the end of next week, with my new purchases to Walmer (the official residence of Mr. Pitt, as Warden of the Cinque Ports), where I am going very shortly. You may imagine I am not a little happy in having it in my power to scamper upon British ground, although I was extremely pleased with my tour, and charmed with Italy.

"I saw a good deal of your friend Capel at Naples; if he fights the battles of his country by sea as well as he fights yours by land, he certainly is one of our first commanders. But of him you must have heard so full an account from Lord Althorp, for they were inseparable, that I will only add he was as yet unsuccessful in the important research after a perfect snuff-box when I left Italy. What news the last dispatch may have brought upon this subject I am ignorant of, but take it for granted you are not; as in all probability the *Phoebe* was, by your interest, appointed to the Mediterranean station for three years, to accomplish this grand and useful discovery. Should it prove a successful one, Capel, on his return, will of course be made Admiral of the *White*, for the signal services he has rendered to coxcombality.

"I met with a rival of yours in affectation upon the

Continent, William Hill! I fear it will be long ere this country will again witness his airs, as he is now a prisoner; this, perhaps, you are glad of, as the society of statues and pictures has infinitely improved him in this wonted qualification, and therefore rendered him a still more formidable competitor.

"HESTER L. STANHOPE."

It is evident that Lady Hester knew Brummell very well: in this letter she disarms him at the outset, and we can be sure that in his reply he responded with gusto to her and his own fearless dexterity in lashing their mutual friends and acquaintances.

No one ever knew why Lady Hester did expatriate and retire to the mountains of Lebanon, living in the most complete seclusion and associating only with Arabs: was it for love? And if so, was it for Beau Brummell? Certain it is that in her solitude Lady Hester still remembered Brummell, even as late as the year 1830. An officer of the Fleet, then serving in the Mediterranean, spent a leave in wandering through Palestine and the adjacent countries, and paid a visit to the "old lady of the mountain". Lady Hester received him graciously, for he was the bearer of a letter from an old friend. At the hour named for the "audience", the officer was admitted by a little black female slave, possibly mute, for the slave ushered him in perfect silence into an apartment so dark that he could scarcely see the ottoman on which a voice at the end of the room desired him to be seated. Then a very small latticed window near him was suddenly opened, and the light fell fully upon him leaving, however, the other end of the apartment in darkness. When his eyes became somewhat accustomed, he saw a woman sitting in oriental fashion on a praying-rug, dressed in Eastern style, and by her side the black slave who had escorted him. Lady Hester inquired after the Duke of Wellington, and then asked the officer for news of George Brummell —these two being the only persons of her country for whom she seemed to entertain any interest. The officer gave in a letter to Captain Jesse an animated description of his visit to Lady Hester at her wild retreat in the Lebanon:

"Many years have passed since I was in Syria; but, as you desire it, I will endeavour to describe my visit to Lady Hester Stanhope as well as my memory permits. I was furnished with a letter of introduction from Lord ——, which I sent from Sidon; a knowledge of her disinclination to receive Englishmen generally having prevented my delivering it personally when passing near her abode on my way from Damascus. Her ladyship, however, acknowledged the letter most politely, invited me and my companion to visit her for as long a time as we found it convenient, and sent two fine Arabian horses to convey us to her residence, which was formerly a convent, and crowns the summit of a hill about eight miles from Sidon.

"The ascent to Mar Elias (for so the convent is called) was steep, and the approach to it more like that of a crusading baron's castle than of the residence of a solitary lady, whose education had been finished, and early habits formed, amongst the most refined and intellectual of the English nobility. A strong guard of Albanians protected the gate, and numbers of armed men, of the same nation, were idling about, as if time was a heavy burthen on their hands. We were conducted to a kiosk or summer house, outside the main building, and there an Italian, dressed like an Arab, received us and provided dinner in the

European fashion; this last appeared to be a matter of some difficulty, as her ladyship conformed to the Eastern habits, in eating, dress, and other matters, and some time had elapsed since plates and forks had been called into requisition. During dinner, an Arab, who spoke French most volubly, made his appearance and told us he was her ladyship's astrologer, and enlarged upon her good fortune in possessing so talented a wizard as himself.

"Soon after, Lady Hester sent to say she would be happy to receive us; and we were accordingly ushered through several apartments, by various attendants, until we reached a small and rather dark room, in which sat her ladyship, dressed as an Arab sheik, and looking more like a young man than an elderly lady. She sat with her back to the light, which streamed in through a small window full on our faces; this she afterwards told me was arranged on purpose to give her a fair scrutiny of the faces of her visitors: chibouques (the long cherry-stick pipe) were introduced, and in a short time she became most agreeably communicative.

"Her conversation was more than ordinarily eloquent, though tinctured with somewhat of the strangeness that pervaded her whole life and character: her thorough knowledge of the language, habits, and customs of the East, combined with the ease with which she expressed her ideas, enabled her to draw the most vivid pictures of those countries, and convey her information in a very agreeable manner. Nor was her conversation by any means confined to these subjects; for when trifling circumstances recalled her thoughts to the days of her youth, when she presided at Mr. Pitt's table, she described those scenes, and the persons of such as were admitted to the circle of her uncle's society, as faithfully and minutely as if the memory of them had not been overlaid by the eight-

and-twenty years she had passed amidst the exciting events of her later life.

"Beau Brummell, who was in her youthful days the friend of the Prince of Wales, and envied and admired by both beaux and belles of all ranks of society, appeared to have been an especial favourite of hers; and though I am unable to repeat the description as she gave it, I can, even now, fancy that I see him riding up to her in the park in a suit of plum-coloured clothes, to give her a stick of perfume of his own manufacture; a peculiar mark of favour, granted only on condition that she promised faithfully not to give a morsel to the Prince, who was dying to get some.

"I hinted at Brummell's eccentricities; but she replied that he was an exceedingly clever man, always suiting his conversation to his hearers, and that he almost always paid her the compliment of talking very sensibly. She added that she had once rebuked him for some folly or other, and inquired why so clever a person as he was did not devote his talents to a higher purpose than he did? To which Brummell replied, that he knew human nature well, and that he had adopted the only course which could place him in a prominent light, and enable him to separate himself from the society of the ordinary herd of men, whom he held in considerable contempt. These conversations, with the attendant chibouque, which her ladyship smoked as determinedly as the longest-bearded Mussulman in the land, were generally prolonged until near daylight, when we retired to rest."

The officer gave this description of Lady Hester at the time of his visit:

"She must have been a tall woman, but her male attire

took off from her height; she was slight, well-formed, and carried herself exceedingly well. The folds of her turban concealed her grey hairs; and the fairness of her complexion, the absence of beard, the brightness of her eye and the vivacity of her expression, gave her the appearance of a young man. Her enunciation was rapid and fluent; and when excited she seemed to light up, and she used her chibouque much in the same way that a Spanish lady uses her fan, except that her gestures were more often those of command than of entreaty. She rode as a man, and was always well armed."

This was, therefore, the Brummell the ladies loved: one cannot think of Brummell as a married man, even less as a paterfamilias. His part upon the stage of fashion would have been marred, nay ruined, by such an emotion as love. Like the Gods of Mythology, Brummell descended from the Olympus to bring anew to men the gift of elegance—the bearer of such a gift could only be a god-like creature enclosed in a brittle shell of supreme egotism that no human passion could scratch. He often wrote of the "transitory sentiment" we call love; he often and easily wrote with a "crow-quill" of "its feigned regrets by tears made with a sponge and rose-water upon perfumed paper"; but did he ever sincerely love? We do not know. There is one strange letter of Miss Georgiana Seymour to Brummell:

"I am more obliged to you than I can express for your note; be assured that your approbation of my conduct has given me very sincere pleasure. This is the only means I have of telling you so, for I am in such disgrace that I do not know if I shall be taken to the play; in any case, I shall be watched: therefore accept my most cordial thanks, and believe that I shall remember your good nature to me on this occasion with gratitude to the end of my life.

"—— does not yet know how unkindly I have been treated, but is more affectionate than ever, because he sees I am unhappy. We did not arrive in town till seven last night. Tomorrow they go to Covent Garden, and perhaps I may be allowed to be one of the party.

"Please don't neglect my drawing: you would make me very happy by lending me the yellow book again; the other I didn't dare ask for, much as I wish for it. Adieu! I shall be steady in my opinion of you, and always remain yours very sincerely,

"GEORGIANA A. F. SEYMOUR."

What service had Brummell rendered to Miss Georgiana Seymour that she should be grateful to him for his approbation of her conduct? Was it a case of his gracefully retiring so as to allow her to obey parental wishes for another engagement with the person who is left unnamed in the letter?

Long after he had received this letter Brummell wrote in a corner of it: "This beautiful creature is dead." And he himself was, then, in the throes of misery and not far distant from death.

Brummell generally preferred the society of married women whose greater knowledge of the world made them more amusing; and his indifference to *bonnes fortunes* made him the idol of women, for women are usually enamoured of men who do not run after them.

Brummell was a marvellous talker; he could draw and paint in water-colours very creditably, and a certain poetical vein allowed him to take no mean part in the fashionable exchanging of *vers de société*.

Brummell kept an album. It was the period when gentlemen and ladies loved to paste things and pieces of papers on the large pages of albums or on the folds of a screen: Byron's screen of what we now call "press cuttings" is a revered museum piece.

The wreck of Caen felt a pang in his heart: why had he given to that heartless Mademoiselle de St. Ursain his precious album? It was, that album, his last tangible link with the past—it was his very self, that ponderous quarto-volume, of plain and stout vellum paper with gilt edges and bound in dark blue velvet, with clasps and corners of massive silver and embossed like the corners of an old missal. In this album Brummell had gathered autographs and famous signatures; it came to contain two hundred and twenty-six pieces of poetry given to him by his friends and some of his own composition; and the choice of the subjects reveals many facets of Brummell's nature, for they are not at all consistent with a worldly and selfish disposition, many of them are descriptive of the characteristics of childhood, in which certainly no one would suspect Brummell of ever having interested himself.

The whole contents seem to have been kept as they were sent to him, either in notes or on loose scraps of paper, and either pasted in or copied in at different periods, for they are arranged so exactly as to avoid turning over a page in any one of them. This album is a little monument of industry; the poetry is inserted by Brummell's hand and the writing is remarkably neat, almost ladylike in its delicacy of penmanship and regularity; as legible as print. What it contains was written in his happy days; and to turn over the pages of this album is to see at a glance to what an extent Brummell's life was linked with that of his best known contemporaries: Byron, Sheridan, the Duchess of Devonshire, the Lords Erskine and John Townshend, Lord Melbourne, Lady Dacre, Lady Granville, the Duchess of York.

Two pieces of verse from his hand occupy one page of the album: the first seems to have been composed for a girl who had taken an oath upon a lock of hair, and the second seems to apply to the same person, as it deals with a similar oath, and the author complains of cruel treachery. And there are some stanzas that Brummell, in later years, asserted were his likewise.

> *Unhappy child of indiscretion,*
> *Poor slumberer on a breast forlorn!*
> *Pledge and reproof of past transgression,*
> *Dear, though unwelcome to be born.*
>
> *For thee, a suppliant wish addressing*
> *To Heaven, thy mother fain would dare;*
> *But conscious blushes stain the blessing,*
> *And sighs suppress my broken prayer:*
>
> *Yet, spite of these, my mind unshaken,*
> *In parent duty turns to thee;*
> *Though long repented, ne'er forsaken,*
> *Thy days shall loved and guarded be!*
>
> *And though to rank and place a stranger,*
> *Thy life an humble course must run:*
> *Still shalt thou learn to fly the danger*
> *Which I, too late, have learnt to shun.*
>
> *And, lest the injurious world upbraid thee,*
> *For mine, or for thy father's ill;*
> *A nameless mother still shall aid thee—*
> *A hand unseen protect thee still.*

Meanwhile, in these sequester'd valleys
· Still shalt thou rest in calm content;
For innocence may smile at malice,
And thou—oh! thou art innocent!

Brummell, in his later years, told the lady to whom he sent a copy of those verses that "he wrote them in 1806 for Julia Storer, who died, most unhappy, some years after".

XII

All biographers have been insistent that George Brummell was not a Dandy—and if we confine our judgment to outward appearances, it is true that Brummell
discarded in his dress all the eccentricities and exaggera-
tions that had been typical of the Dandies. But the very
essence of George Brummell, his philosophy of life, his
whole attitude to life and society was that of a born-
Prince of Dandyism.

What is Dandyism? It is most difficult to define. For
Dandyism is something both ephemeral and eternal; and
even in the shabby epoch in which we live, without a
single shred left of an inclination, not to say a concern,
for elegance in the true sense, Dandyism survives; it survives, happily, in the approach to life, in the manner of
living of a few men who will hand the torch to other men,
from epoch to epoch—for the spirit of Petronius Arbiter
is as immortal and unextinguishable as the spirit of Plato
and Leonardo.

What then, is Dandyism? It is something both human
and intellectual. It is compounded of vanity, a base sentiment indeed, and of ambition, which is the strongest
impulse to greatness. But ambition can be fulfilled only
by action, and action is seldom elegant. And pride can
go hand-in-hand with selfishness and unkindness. Vanity
is neither selfish nor unkind; indeed, she thrives on good
manners and kindness. The vain is seldom fatuous. A vain
man is a flower that expects to be watered by the dew of
admiration. Such is the Dandy.

It is not enough to be dressed to perfection to be a Dandy. One may be a Dandy in a creased suit. Indeed, incredible as it may seem, the Dandies once had a fancy for torn clothes: to invent new originality some Dandies had the impertinence, and certainly the bad taste, to walk about in clothes that were torn before wearing them; the absurd operation being performed with a piece of pointed glass.

Probably the origin of Dandyism was French. But the word Dandyism has no equivalent in any other language; and we must take it, therefore, that Dandyism is a truly English interpretation of a philosophy of life. Only England has provided a genuine Dandy—George Brummell; all other countries have only had a crop of imitators, often second-rate.

Elegance had returned to England at the Restoration of Charles II, leaning on the arms of corruption. Elegance came to attack the seriousness of Cromwell's Protestants, whose high-mindedness was rooted in bad manners. The greatest merit of Charles II's Court will most certainly remain that of having helped England to escape from the tyranny of bad manners if not of so-called morality.

Every great event in history occurs in its proper time, and the England of Charles II was most anxious to be corrupted. Men like Rochester and Shaftesbury strode a century ahead of French manners and reached the Regency at one bound. And there were Buckingham and Hamilton and Charles himself. These men began the reign of the Beaux. The Beaux are not to be confused with the Dandies, whom they precede. Dandyism was already existing below the surface, for Dandyism is as old as civilization; but it was to spring from the heart of society. "Handsome Fielding"—as Charles II called him—died in 1712, succeeded by Colonel Edgeworth; the chain of

Beaux closed with Nash, and opened the door to Brummell escorted by Dandyism. The interval between Fielding and Nash marked the period of its development and concretion.

The name Dandyism was given later. We do not find it in Johnson's Dictionary; yet Dandyism existed at that time. Marlborough, Chesterfield, Bolingbroke, all were tinged with incipient Dandyism. It was indeed Chesterfield who made of his letters the Treatise of the Gentleman, not so much by prescribing the Laws as by detailing the customs of the estate. Chesterfield is still tightly bound to accepted opinion; Marlborough, with his beauty like a haughty lady's, has about him more of avarice than of amity. Bolingbroke alone is advanced, a real Dandy of the later days. He has all the boldness of action, the sumptuous impertinence, the pre-occupation of the effect, and his vanity is ever on the alert. Breaking through the prudery of London drawing-rooms, did he not advertise his very natural love for an orange-girl, perhaps not even pretty, who stood under the galleries of Parliament? And it was Bolingbroke who invented the motto of Dandyism, *Nil mirari*, do not wonder at anything, be as the gods who surprise us by remaining impassive.

A Dandy was to be calm, impassive. Were a Dandy to speak like Pericles, he would keep his arms folded under his cloak. Rulhière, who treated history as an anecdote, tells us of the Russian Princess d'Aschekoff who scandalized the Court by not wearing rouge, when red in Russia meant beautiful, so much so that the very beggars did not dare to practise their calling without being rouged. The non-rouge of Princess d'Aschekoff was pure Dandyism. A true Dandy was the Austrian Prince de Kaunitz, not for his calm and his nonchalance and indifference and ferocious egoism, but because in order to get his hair powdered exactly to the right shade, he passed through a suite of drawing-rooms whose size and numbers he had calculated, and was powdered as he passed by footmen armed with puffs.

Dandyism is a complete theory of life. It is a philosophy of life, made up entirely of shades, of things that are utterly unessential, such as the things and ways that compose a very civilized society.

The Dandies made rules that dominated the most aristocratic and the most conservative, and imposed these rules with the help of wit, which is an acid, and of grace, which is a solvent. In vain do Democracies admit only regimented opinions; one day Caprice will arise and make its way again through the impenetrable glades. For these rules are eternal, and they escape the warfare of vulgar men. The rules of Dandyism are the science of manners and attitudes, a science which thrives in the garden of frivolity and imagination: and frivolities are the only things that really matter in life. George Brummell was the final expression of this, and he will never be equalled.

At the zenith of his success, Brummell was the hero of elegant idleness. He had no keen interest in the world outside himself, and quite rightly he found a greater interest in beautiful snuff-boxes than in social questions. In this he was the true Dandy, for Dandyism is the art of selection, practised by a lover of the visible world. Only when one rises above the dreariness of the Rights of Man can one be a true Dandy: and this rise implies a strength of character not inferior to the duel between the Archangel and Lucifer.

Brummell's philosophy of life was, like his elegance, heaven-born—he could be charmingly familiar without profaning the proportions; he was safe where abler men would have been lost. And Brummell's whole life was an influence, which is something ordinary men find difficult to understand: for an influence is something we feel all the time it lasts, and when it ceases to be we note its value by the difference. An influence is like time remembered. English society of Brummell's time, shaped by Brummell, so detailed and clever, is not to be rediscovered.

The empire ruled by Brummell was a realm of personal autocracy. And the marvel is that the facts of Brummell's life, which have entirely perished, have nothing in themselves to justify such admiration, because they would be called ephemeral: but are manners ephemeral? Are they not the only thing that we really remember of past history, far more and far nearer our hearts and minds than the so-called great deeds?

It was by his manners that Brummell became a prince of his times, and his name remains, like the names of the famous orators, the actors, the artists, the names of all the men who spoke to us through our mind and senses. We cannot explain the place Brummell fills in history; but the mere mention of his name brings to our minds the lustre of his person and of his manners. He was an exception, and it is difficult to describe exactly that influence which answers to an exception, and turns exception into a law and a conception of life.

During his lifetime a strange portrait of him was drawn: Granby, by Trebeck. A few light strokes drawn by a quill on bluish paper with silver margin. A mere frivolity dipped in Chinese ink. The curious touches of Trebeck must have been drawn from life; they are beyond invention. Or perhaps we may recognize Brummell in Bulwer's novel *Pelham*. Yet, Brummell still lacks an historical explanation. Fame reflected him in the sparkling purity of her brittle surface, and at the back of the changeable mirror of Fashion we can still see the image of Brummell.

There was in Brummell a harmony between nature and destiny, between genius and fortune. His mind was not great; he was not destined to leave behind, like Byron, immortal works. His destiny was to be a Dandy, the perfect Dandy, and he fulfilled his destiny admirably—he was Dandyism personified.

PART TWO

Arbiter Elegantiarum

I

The years went by. In the "reign" of George Brum-mell over London society there were no events to record. It was, day in, day out, the life of a gentleman. Gentlemen, in those days, did not work; it was, in fact, ungentlemanly to work. One could write a book or compose poems, as several did; or one could devote oneself to politics. But no gentleman did any work for his living, at least in the sense we do it nowadays. This is perhaps the great difference between the past and the present; yet, the past did stretch well into the nineteenth century and it is within the memory of the living that men who did work and even those who attained notable success with their work had to strive very hard to be admitted into society; we all remember how many London clubs, in the 1920's, still barred from membership gentlemen who were "in trade" or did any business. The life of a gentleman in Brummell's time was not much different from a gentle-man's life in London in that modern world that came to an end in 1939. One attended to one's *toilette* and appearance with due care; one rode in the park or played golf; lunched at the fashionable places; gambled or betted; did some visiting and spent the evening at a show and afterwards went to parties in fashionable houses. Substitute the club's dining-room for the restaurant, the assembly rooms for the night-clubs, and we have the same kind of life.

Brummell read a great deal, his letters are full of allusions to the current books. He collected Sèvres porcelain and pieces of Buhl furniture, and he put together also a fair collection of prints and drawings. In a letter dated

1800 he wrote to a friend: "I am quite unhappy that I have no more drawings to send you, and I have equally to regret my inability to plead any better excuse for the poverty of my *portefeuille* than my natural idleness and the deprecation of my friends."

Now and then he wrote a piece of poetry. After the death of the Duchess Georgiana of Devonshire there appeared in the *Gentleman's Magazine* a fantasy in verse for children. *The Butterfly's Ball*, by William Roscoe the historian, famous for his accounts of Lorenzo Il Magnifico and Leo X. The verses charmed many people, and by order of the King and Queen were set to music for the Princess Mary. Brummel had an inspiration, and wrote the counterpart, *The Butterfly's Funeral*, meant for children too, but it is possible to surmise that in the poem he grieved over the loss of his friend the Duchess of Devonshire: she was the Butterfly and he might be discerned in the Grasshopper; the scenes bore the reminiscence and the colour of the gatherings at Chatsworth and Devonshire House.

> *Oh ye! who so lately were blythesome and gay,*
> *At the Butterfly's banquet carousing away;*
> *Your feasts and your revels of pleasure are fled,*
> *For the soul of the banquet, the Butterfly's dead!*
>
> *No longer the Flies and the Emmets advance,*
> *To join with their friend in the Grasshopper's dance;*
> *For see his thin form o'er the favourite bend,*
> *And the Grasshopper mourns for the loss of his friend.*
>
> *And hark! to the funeral dirge of the Bee,*
> *And the Beetle, who follows as solemn as he;*
> *And see where so mournful the green rushes wave,*
> *The Mole is preparing the Butterfly's grave.*

The Dormouse attended, but cold and forlorn,
  And the Gnat slowly winded his shrill little horn;
And the Moth, who was grieved for the loss of a sister,
  Bent over the body and silently kiss'd her.

The corse was embalm'd at the set of the sun,
  And enclosed in a case which the Silk-worm had spun;
By the help of the Hornet the coffin was laid
  On a bier out of myrtle and jessamine made.

In weepers and scarves came the Butterflies all,
  And six of their number supported the pall;
And the Spider came there, in his mourning so black,
  But the fire of the Glowworm soon frighten'd him back.

The Grub left his nutshell, to join in the throng,
  And slowly led with him the Bookworm along;
Who wept his poor neighbour's unfortunate doom,
  And wrote these few lines, to be placed on her tomb:

EPITAPH

At this solemn spot, where the green rushes wave,
  Here sadly we bent o'er the Butterfly's grave;
'Twas here we to beauty our obsequies paid,
  And hallow'd the mound which her ashes had made.

And here shall the daisy and violet blow,
  And the lily discover her bosom of snow;
While under the leaf, in the evenings of spring,
  Still mourning his friend, shall the Grasshopper sing.

It was not great poetry, but it was a success: the little
poem was published anonymously by John Wallis in
1807, and it sold three thousand copies, not all to children.

He was fond of drawing and painting in water-colours and made sketches and portraits in pencil, ink and colours: there was quite a good sketch of the Duchess of Devonshire copied in miniature from Reynold's portrait of her. He did not disdain showing his own drawings and sketches to his friends, and once while visiting Ticknell Hall, Lord Granville's home, Brummell was actually mistaken by an old gentleman for an artist! It happened that while the drawings were being handed about by the company in the drawing-room, dinner was announced, and Brummell rose to offer his arm to a lady: an old gentleman who did not know Brummell very well, rose at the same time with the same intention, and the Beau, out of respect for the old man's grey hair promptly withdrew with a bow. The old gentleman, mistaking him for an artist, loudly remarked that he was glad to see "that the young man knew his place!"

One of Brummell's great hobbies, and one which, on his example, became quite a fashion, was to collect snuff-boxes, of which he put together a notable collection. At the time "taking snuff" was quite the thing, and a man of fashion had snuff-boxes for all occasions and dress. The smartest men had a box for every day of the year; others were content with different boxes suitable for the various seasons, or for different hours of the day, or for visiting or travelling. There were devised canes incorporating a snuff-box in the handle. The libertine had boxes shaped like ladies' legs, or decorated in the inside of the lid with saucy vignettes; the vain ones carried boxes with a small mirror inside the lid.

As in everything else, Brummell set the tone in the way of taking snuff. The box was carried constantly in the hand, not only to have it always ready, but also because the weight of a box heavily jewelled and enamelled might spoil the line of a waistcoat. In a *salon*, Brummell's style was this: poised evenly on the two feet, he opened the lid of the box with a flick of the left thumb, with a movement of the whole hand that set in relief his white well-shaped hand and the ring on the middle finger, and the correct amount of shirt-cuffs showing out of his coat sleeves and the embroidered handkerchief of fine cambric. The lady or the gentleman to whom the box was then proffered, would then deign to hold a pose with out-stretched two fingers and take a pinch. If it was a lady, the act of putting the two fingers into the snuff gave her an opportunity for displaying her rings and bracelets and her snowy and well-modelled arm or the frail romantic wrist. The pinch would then be an excuse for a brief pause in the conversation: a moment of suspense, nay, of aspiration. . . . Afterwards the conversation would, inevitably, turn upon the most exquisite aroma and the beauty or novelty of the box. After which the lid would be closed with another little flick of the middle finger of the left hand, with military precision. And the conversation, underlined with delicate, or generous, sneezes and blowing of noses, would skip along upon a rivulet of gossips and topics that did not fatigue the mind.

In the matter of snuff Brummell's opinion was unquestioned. Fribourg and Treyer, whose shop in the Haymarket was patronized by the connoisseurs, were one year anxiously expecting their supply of the veritable Martinique, and the list of applicants for this highly-prized snuff had long been filled. The day came when the hogshead was ceremoniously opened in the presence of the Arbiter, who, after taking a few pinches, gravely pronounced it a detestable compound, and not the style that any man with the slightest pretension to correct taste could

possibly patronize. This astounding announcement petrified the shopkeepers, especially as Brummell's companions
left him in the shop to discuss the matter. But no sooner
were they gone than Brummel said: "By some oversight
I did not put my name down on your Martinique list.
Since the hogshead has been condemned, you will not
object to my having three jars of it; no one knows its
value as I do, and there is little doubt that when I shall
open my box, the remainder will find a speedy demand."
Messrs. Fribourg were only too glad to yield to the ruse
of the exquisite arbiter of fashion. When it became known
that he had absolutely bought and positively paid for
three jars of it, not a grain of the Martinique was left.

"A life of leisure", Brummell said in those days, "is a
most difficult art. One has to cheat continuously the ennui;
and boredom is as depressing as an insistent creditor."

With the passing of time, Brummell, who had enjoyed
inventing the cravat and the trousers with the buttoned
bottom and the evening black coat, abandoned the pre-
occupation of his youth: he continued to dress irreproach-
ably, but his clothes were darker in colour, more simply
cut and worn without concern. In this sense he was the
perfect Dandy, who may spend ten hours a day dressing,
but once dressed thinks no more about it—it is for others
to notice that he is well dressed. Thus Brummell arrived
at the summit of art, where it meets nature. He was still
consulted by his friends about a new style. One day the
Duke of Beaufort met him in St. James's, on the way to
the club, and asked him what he thought of his new coat.
Brummell made him turn this way and the other, and
then he spoke: "Do you call this a coat?" The Duke went
straight back home to change his clothes.

The relations with the Prince of Wales remained quite

intimate. In fact, they had changed, no longer were they the royal patron and the protégé, now they were equals —joint sovereigns of the world that composed their separate Courts. But in matter of dress, Brummell remained the undisputed arbiter. In Brummell's fastidious taste the Prince discerned a more rigid selectivity, that quest for a perfect harmony which he was not fitted by temperament to share, for the Prince leaned too often to the decorative and the lavish and on one occasion, at a parade of troops, he went so far as to add rows of diamonds to his Hussar uniform.

Brummell's point of vantage was the bow-window at White's Club. From that graceful window, that still adorns the club's lovely frontage, Brummell, like a god-of-taste in his fitting shrine, let his words of judgment fall, and the witticisms which were dropped from that window were not always kind. A few years hence Brummell would say to a *nouveau riche* who pressed for the reimbursement of a small loan: "Good Lord! And one day I bowed to you from The Window, and I said 'Hello, Jimmy'!"

Brummell's fascination, however, remained intellectual. His person was distinguished, his features handsome despite the fact that a fall from his horse had marred the Grecian regularity of his profile. But his air was finer than his face, and his bearing surpassed the perfection of his frame. Sometimes there came into his clever, mocking eyes, a look of glacial indifference without contempt, as becomes a man who bears within him something superior to the visible world. His voice remained splendid, his accents and diction were perfect. Those who were not of sufficient importance to his vanity, he would gaze at with calm but wondering eyes. And he pleased with his person as others please with their works.

He maintained an immense influence over other men.

He drew out of its torpidity a society that was essentially blasé; and to effect this he did not sacrifice an inch of his dignity. He was not an amiable man, for there was too much correctness in him to be perfectly amiable. But it was as though his very caprices were respected.

His greatest asset was the genius of irony, which gave him that sphinx-like air which interests us as a mystery and a danger. His genius for irony made him one of the greatest mystificators that England ever possessed. Dandyism is the product of a bored society, and boredom is not conducive to kindness. Brummell preferred astonishing to pleasing, a preference that often succeeds. Less than a century later, Oscar Wilde modelled his life on this preference.

Brummell's indolence forbade his being lively, for to be lively is to be excited, to be excited is to care about something and to care about something is to show oneself inferior: Brummell was always cool and always said the right thing. His witticisms crucified. He did not bubble and sparkle as Oscar Wilde's wit did; he did not try his epigrams upon his friends as Oscar Wilde did before putting them on the lips of characters in his plays; Brummell simply let his witticisms fall from his lips; his impertinence was too great to be condensed into epigrams. It passed from expression into action, attitudes, gestures and inflection of the voice. His wit was of that superior quality which alone is possible in good society, for wit borders on vulgarity as the sublime verges on the ridiculous and one false step is fatal. Impertinence is a veiled genius and does not need the help of words to score; it is a shield against the vanity of others, so often hostile.

So intellectual a power was Brummell, that he ruled even more by what he looked than by what he said. His effect upon others was more direct than the action of speech. He influenced by an intonation, a look, a gesture, by obvious intention, by silence itself. As a great master of conversation, he was often silent; but Brummell's silence was another way of producing effect, it was the tantalizing coquetry of one who is sure of pleasing and knows at which end desire takes fire, and this explains why he has left so few witticisms.

Society rewarded him with all the happiness in its power. There was no fashionable assembly or party where his presence was not regarded as a triumph; his absence was a catastrophe. In the papers his name was printed before those of the most illustrious guests. At Almack's balls and Ascot meetings, everyone bowed beneath his sway. But he had a kindness of his own, a kindness which he made the rule of his life and set as a model to all elegant men. "Civility, my good fellow," he said to a young gentleman who had laid himself open to censure by the thoughtless omission of an act of courtesy to the lady near whom the young man was standing. "Civility may truly be said to cost nothing; if it does not meet with a due return, it at least leaves you in the most creditable position. When I was young, I was acquainted with a striking example of what may sometimes be gained by it, though my friend on this occasion did not, I assure you, expect to benefit by his politeness. In leaving the Opera one evening, a short time previous to the fall of the curtain, he overtook in the lobby an elderly lady, making her way out to avoid the crowd; she was dressed in a most peculiar manner, with hoop and brocade, and a pyramid of hair; in fact, she was at least a century behind the rest of the world in her costume; so singular an apparition had attracted the attention of half a dozen 'Lord Dukes' and 'Sir Harrys', sitting in the lobby, and as she slowly moved towards the box entrance they amused themselves by making impertinent remarks on her extraordinary dress, and infirm gait.

"Directly my friend caught sight of them, and saw what they were after, he went to her assistance, threatened to give them in charge to a Bow Street officer, and with his best bow offered her his arm. She accepted it, and on the stairs he inquired whether she had a chair or a carriage, at the same time intimating his willingness to go for one. 'Thank you, sir, I have my chair,' replied the old lady, 'if you will only be good enough to remain with me until it arrives.' As she was speaking, her servants came up with it, and, making the cavalier a very stately curtsy, she requested to know to whom she had the honour of being indebted for so much attention. 'My name, madam,' replied the stranger, as he handed her to her chair, 'is Boothby, but I am usually called Prince Boothby,' upon which the antiquated lady thanked him once more, and left. Well, from that hour Boothby never saw her again, and did not hear of her till her death, which took place a few years after, when he received a letter from her lawyer, announcing to him the agreeable intelligence of her having left him heir to several thousands a year! Now, my good sir," said Brummell to the abashed but youthful delinquent, "for the future, pray remember Prince Boothby."

II

It was now 1807: the war with "Bony" was flagging. Napoleon was Emperor of France. The blockade of Europe was at its peak. Trade in Britain was prospering on the contraband to Napoleon's Europe. The fight of England against Napoleon—that had started on the 1st February 1793 and was to last, with a brief interval of fifteen months, for twenty-two years—was but the fight of the sea against all the combined forces of the Continent of Europe. And England, which at that time had, including Scotland, less than ten million inhabitants, and never put together more than four hundred thousand men—the maximum ever reached was, in 1802, 404,068—had, however, assembled a fleet whose men numbered, in 1813, nearly one hundred and fifty thousand men. But the blockade had worked in favour of England—England found herself the general shipper for all Europe's needs. In 1806, from Berlin, Napoleon had decreed the blockade of England; but, in reality, the trade of England had risen in one year and had more than doubled, and no part of the Continent could obtain sugar and coffee and spices except through England; in the Mediterranean the Turkish flag on Greek ships was hiding English goods to Trieste, Venice and Genoa; on the Adriatic coast, a firm used five hundred horses to bring English goods into France itself; and English goods entered Europe everywhere in boats and barges, under women's skirts, even inside the coffins of mock funerals! England was growing rich and London life was even more hectic than ever.

One night in 1807, after dinner at Carlton House, the Prince inquired of some members of White's and Brooks's, who were present, what sort of fare they got at their clubs. Sir Thomas Stapley answered: "The eternal joint and beef-steaks, the boiled fowl with oyster sauce, and an apple tart. That is what we have, sir, and very monotonous fare it is." His Royal Highness nodded understandingly, rang for his chef, Watier, and asked him if he would care to take a house and organize a club, where special attention should be given to the cuisine. Watier liked the idea and named Madison, the Prince's page, as manager, and Labourier, from Carlton House, as chief cook. "You, Brummell," said the Prince, "can make this your own club." It was, there and then, decided to call the new club "Watier's". A house was soon found at No. 81 Piccadilly, at the east corner of Bolton Street. The house had been for some time the headquarters of a group of gentlemen, headed by Lord Headford and John Maddocks, who used it for their hobby of singing glees, catches and madrigals—they called them "harmonic meetings".

George Brummell was elected permanent President. There is in existence a letter from Byron to Lady Blessington which tells us about Watier's: "In my time Watier's was the Dandy Club, of which, though no dandy, I was a member; at that time, too, of its greatest glory, when Brummell, Mildmay, Alvanley and Pierrepoint gave the Dandy Balls; and we, that is, the Club, got up the famous masquerade at Burlington House and Garden for Wellington." Byron not only liked the club, but liked the Dandies: "They were always very civil to me, though in general they disliked literary people, and mystified Madame de Staël and the like, damnably. The truth is that, though I gave up the business early, I had a tinge of dandyism in my minority, and probably retained enough of it to conciliate the great one, at four-and-twenty. I knew them all more or less, and they made me a member of Watier's, a superb club at that time, being, I take it, the only literary man, except two others, both men of the world, Moore and Sheridan in it."

At Watier's Brummell was the supreme dictator. He gave much of his time to the club, supervising the perfection of the appointments, on the lookout for the slightest flaw, always urbane, witty and polished, courted by all and feared by many, laying down the law on dress, on manners and on those magnificent and costly snuff-boxes that were all the rage. The Prince of Wales did not use the club; but his brother, the Duke of York, joined it. Watier's became a kind of Court for Brummell, and he fomented the excesses, ridiculed the scruples, patronized the novices and exercised paramount dominion over all.

The dinners at Watier's were most exclusive; the most exquisite dinners were supplied, and it was a rule not to charge the card-players for their dinner, so that Watier's soon became a place of constant play, Macao being the favourite game, and gambling became so heavy that few could stay the pace. One night Tom Sheridan came into the club and, although not an habitual gambler, laid £10 at Macao. Brummell happened to drop in from the Opera at the moment, and proposed that he should take Sheridan's place, promising to go half with him in any winnings he might collect. Brummell's luck at the moment was phenomenal; the Beau added £200 to his friend's modest stake, and in ten minutes had won £1,500. Here he stopped and handing £750 to Sheridan remarked: "There, Tom, go home and give your wife and brats a supper, and never play again."

Brummell now gave up his old rooms in Chesterfield Street, and moved a few blocks away, between Grosvenor

Square and Park Lane, into more spacious rooms, at 24 South Street. In South Street was the house in which Charles James Fox had spent his last years, although he had died in the Duke of Devonshire's house in Chiswick.

Brummell was wrong in leaving the rooms in Chesterfield Street: within those old rooms there were all the memories of the years when he had made his conquest of London Society. And soon after he had left Chesterfield Street, Lady Hester Stanhope left England for ever. Her departure had nothing to do with him; for Lady Hester had been in love with General Sir John Moore, who fell in Spain at the battle of Corunna, with her name on his lips; and Lady Hester went away from England in deep mourning. But with the departure of the lovely and impudent Lady Hester Stanhope there ceased for Brummell the merry passages of wit, for Lady Hester was a charming influence in Brummell's life, the other good influence being Georgiana Devonshire, and she had already gone.

III

In the autumn of the same year that Brummell lost the steadying friendship of Lady Hester Stanhope, the youngest daughter of King George III, the Princess Amelia, died of consumption; sending her father a ring which contained a lock of her hair and which was engraved with the message: "Remember me when I am gone." The last message of his beloved caused a recurrence of madness in the old king, and within three months a Regency Bill was passed by Parliament, and in February the Prince of Wales became Regent. The fact was to be of much importance in the life of George Brummell.

The madness of King George III was of a strange nature. In the months preceding the Regency he was visited at Windsor Castle by the Reverend John Evans of Islington, who described the King as neatly dressed, in blue coat with gilt buttons and blue star, white waistcoat, white stockings and gold buckles on his shoes. His hat resembled that worn by the clergy, with the addition of a gold button and loop, mounted by a black cockade. He looked ruddy and full; his voice was sonorous and he conversed with cheerfulness. During the visit he inquired about the balloon in which Sadler the aeronaut had made his ascent; touched his hat and said: "Gentlemen, good night," to the band of musicians on the steps of the terrace, and chatted affably with the ladies and gentlemen who withdrew on either side at his passage, kept in check by a police officer with a little switch, and ended the day playing on the harpsichord, an instrument that had formerly belonged to the great Handel and was supposed to have been manufactured at Antwerp in the year 1612.

Anyway, on the 11th January 1811—and the year had come in bitterly cold, with sad tales in consequence—a delegation of the Commons went, in great state, to the Prince of Wales and a delegation of the Lords went to the Queen, to inform them that the Prince was appointed Regent. The Prince replied very solemnly, calling on the "Divine Will to extricate us, and the nation, from the grievous embarrassments of our present condition."

The fat and gay Prince of Wales felt that he must emulate the knights of old, who spent the eve of their knighthood in vigil and prayers and guarding their armour; and so, before he became Prince Regent, he partook of the Holy Eucharist, albeit the sole object of his piety was to obtain a certificate that he was in the communion of the Church of England. Nevertheless this public act of worship was a stately affair; the Prince was in the Royal Closet during the major portion of the service, and afterwards, attended by three lords, he went up to the altar, took his seat under a canopy, made his offering in a gold dish, and then, with the three attendant lords, took Holy Communion.

On the 6th of February the Prince was sworn-in as Regent. The ceremony was a great one. About twelve o'clock a party of the flank companies of Grenadiers, with their colours, the bands and drums and fifes, with white garters, marched into the courtyard of Carlton House, pitched their colours in the centre of the grand entrance; the band struck up "God Save the King", and continued playing the anthem alternately with martial airs until five o'clock. Six Yeomen of the Guard and an usher, together with the Prince's servants in state, lined the grand hall and staircase, and several of the rooms; at three o'clock

the Duke of Montrose, followed by all the royal dukes and
an assembly of Privy Councillors, arrived, and the magnificent suite of state apartments were opened and the
illustrious persons were ushered into the Gold Room: the
Prince approached in grand procession preceded by the
officers of his household.

They passed through the Circular Drawing-room (circular rooms were then the height of elegance), and from
this into the grand *salon*, which was draped in scarlet,
embellished with portraits of the admirals who had fought
the battles that had given England the dominion of the
seas; and here the Prince seated himself at the top of the
table, with his royal brothers and cousins on each side,
whilst the officers of the household ranged themselves on
each side of the entrance to the room. Then, the Privy
Councillors, in full dress, and according to their rank,
headed by the Archbishop of Canterbury, the Lord
Chancellor, the Archbishop of York and the Lord President, made their reverence to the Prince, who made a
graceful return to each, and they took their place at the
table: and at last the Prince delivered his speech interspersed with "So help me, God", and subscribed the two
oaths.

Afterwards he handed to the President of the Council
a certificate of his having received the Sacrament of the
Lord's Supper at the Chapel Royal of St. James, and the
Lord President approached the Regent, bent the knee,
and kissed his hand. The royal dukes followed and so did
the archbishops and all the rest. During the whole of the
ceremony His Royal Highness maintained, it was remarked, the most graceful and dignified deportment.

The next event was a grand fête given by the Prince to
two thousand of the Nobility and Gentry and Foreign
Ambassadors at Carlton House. For fully six weeks tailors,

milliners and mantua-makers worked for it, while archi-
tects, painters, carpenters, upholsterers, cooks and con-
fectioners contrived to make the Regent's fête splendid:
diamonds were borrowed by ladies and gentlemen for the
night at 11 per cent.

The fête took place on the 19th of June. The whole of
Carlton House, even the basements, which were utilized
as supper rooms, were thrown open to the guests, and a
large portion of the garden was used for supper. The
Throne-room was splendidly hung with crimson velvet,
embroidered in pure gold, with massive fringes. The
canopy, carved and gilt, was surmounted by four helmets
of real gold, with white plumes of the finest ostrich feathers,
seventeen inches high. On each side of the canopy were
magnificent antique draperies, forming a background to
two superb candelabra, and under the canopy stood a
grand State-chair and foot-stool. The compartments of
the room were decorated with the richest gold ornaments
on a crimson velvet; there were two superb mirrors about
twelve feet high, resting upon oriental alabaster tables on
gilt frames. On a chimney, decorated with ormolu foliage,
was placed a mirror in a superb frame; and on the chimney-piece and tables were fine French girandoles of
ormolu. In this room there were no other seats than stools,
gilt and covered with crimson velvet, as was proper in the
presence of the Regent representing the Throne. Through
a door at one end of this room a temporary staircase had
been erected as a private passage for the Prince and his
particular friends to pass down to the head of the tables
when supper was announced. A door leading to the
Throne-room had been removed, and a large mirror
being placed in the opposite door, beyond the throne,
the whole range of candelabra and the throne itself were
reflected in it with a striking effect.

The ballroom was decorated with Arabesque ornaments and figures, forerunners of the Brighton Pavilion
that the Regent was planning to rebuild in grander style.
The windows and recesses in that room had circular tops,
and these were decorated with blue velvet draperies,
again adorned with massive gold fringes, lace tassels and
ropes; and in the recesses were tall French mirrors in
gold frames with sofas under them. Before each pilaster
was a richly gilt pedestal, on which stood a superb French
girandole in ormolu carrying eight wax lights; and the
statuary on the two chimney-pieces was profusely ornamented with ormolu, and over them were mirrors in gold
frames and candelabra of ormolu. The whole decoration
of Carlton House for the fête was indeed the apotheosis of
velvet draperies and gilt.

The Regent entered the apartments at a quarter past
nine, dressed in a scarlet coat most richly ornamented,
in a very novel style, with gold lace and a brilliant Star
of the Garter, and he arrived—oh, strange coincidence!
—just at the same time as the dethroned Louis XVIII,
who was in England as the Comte de Lille. Dancing began
about twelve, and at half-past two supper was announced.
At no Court in Europe had ever been served a sit-down
supper for two thousand people. The largest entertainment, at the most brilliant period of the French Court,
had been the fête given by the Prince of Condé at Chan-
tilly, in honour of the King of Sweden, when four hundred
covers were laid. One thousand six hundred of the
Regent's two thousand guests sat under canvas in the
gardens, and four hundred sat in the house. In the gardens there were three walks, which crossed the broad and
lofty wall adjoining St. James's Park. These walks were
closed in by walls and covered by awnings, under which
ran long supper tables, and at the end of each walk was

erected a circular marquee for the service. The sides of the walls were covered with festoons of flowers, relieved by verdant plants and shrubs. From the arched roofs were suspended thousands of lights: the sight from the central entrance to the gardens was delightful—an Arabian night's dream. Some lampoonist called it a Neronian banquet.

The Conservatory, which was in Gothic style, had a circular buffet surmounted by a medallion with the initial G.P.R. lined by festoons and draperies of pink and silver, and partly filled by mirrors before which, upon ornamented shelves, stood the most exquisite gold plate. At the head table in this splendid supper-room sat the Regent, and in front of his seat was a circular basin of water, with a Temple in the centre of it, from which a meandering stream ran to the bottom of the table, bordered with green banks. Three or four fantastic bridges were thrown over it, one of them with a small tower, which gave the little stream a picturesque appearance. In the stream there were also gold and silver fishes. It was beautiful and charming; and the gold and silver pieces were used with a grandeur and good taste that was beautiful and superb.

And the ladies' dresses and gentlemen's arrays put the *Vielle Cour de Versailles* into shade. The servants themselves wore a rich costume of dark blue trimmed with very broad gold lace. The assistants wore black suits and white vests. Two bands of the Guards played throughout the night.

The ladies had been requested to dress in the products of British industry: the Marchioness of Devonshire exceeded all others in splendour, wearing a petticoat of white satin trimmed at the bottom with a Spanish net of embossed silver, over which was a tunic of the most beautiful silver stuff of Irish manufacture, on which was woven the shamrock; over the shoulders she wore superb epaulettes of embossed Spanish silver; the tunic was laced with diamond chains, and fastened in front with large diamond brooches: the ear-rings were the largest diamonds at the fête, with a corresponding necklace and a profusion of diamond ornaments.

IV

Knowing the proclivities of the Prince, it was imagined that the Regent would give places to all his entourage, and the caricature of "Robing the Prince or the Road to Preferment" showed Earl Grey and Grenville and Sheridan.

But Brummell received no "preferment", no sinecure. Strangely enough, with the elevation of the Prince to the Regency, he seemed to find pleasure in affecting marked criticism of his royal friend.

The Prince was becoming more amorous and polygamous than ever, and gross to the point of ridicule. Although Mrs. Fitzherbert still retained her position of morganatic wife, the Prince now was pursuing the elderly Marchioness of Hertford. In fact, he had always showed an inclination towards women who were mature mothers if not grandmothers. Lady Hertford was of plump contours, but not as fat as Mrs. Fitzherbert; and she was much haughtier. She lived with her husband in Manchester Square, in the house which now contains the Wallace Collection. With a peculiar touch of delicacy, the Prince had given her as a token of love the Reynolds's portraits of "Perdita" Robinson, who had been his old flame a generation before: some said that it was this now famous portrait that encouraged the Hertfords, with their £150,000 a year, in the collecting passion. Another queer side of his ardour for Lady Hertford was that at every dinner party he gave for her, the Regent expected Mrs. Fitzherbert to attend.

And soon Lady Hertford was succeeded by Lady Bessborough—who had hazel eyes, glossy auburn hair, pearly teeth and was a grandmother! It was whispered that the fat ardent lover, rolling his huge belly from the couch upon the floor, endeavoured to conquer her with the arm of politics, and as Lady Bessborough had sworn that she would yield to his love only if he would make Canning Prime Minister, he kept repeating "Canning—Canning!" and reached with his paws for the auburn-haired grandmother.

It was known at Carlton House that Brummell was making jokes about all this. Did Brummell think that his power was as great as the Prince's? Did he feel that the Regency rested on two men: the Regent and Mr. George Brummell equally resplendent and sovereigns? In Brummell's mind they were not Prince and subject, Patron and Beau—they were one gentleman to another. Had not a few days previously, the Prince, looking over Brummell's superb collection of snuff-boxes at his rooms in South Street, taken such a fancy to one that he had exclaimed: "Ah, Brummell, I really think this box must be mine; go to Gray's and order any box you like in lieu of it." And he, Brummell had suggested that he might have one with the Prince's miniature upon the lid, to which the Regent readily assented. And Brummell had designed the box himself, with the portrait set around with diamonds. It was to be a generous memento from the Prince in return for the exquisite box which Brummell had surrendered. Indeed, when the miniature was partly executed, the Prince himself suggested some improvements and alterations, and the work of the jewellers went on.

Yes, the Regent could not do without Brummell—the gross and babbling Prinny needed, for the lustre of his Court, his own Petronius. And if Brummell disapproved, now and then, of Mrs. Fitzherbert, why should he not do so? Had he not been *chevalier d'honneur* at the Prince's wedding to the unhappy Princess of Wales?

But Mrs. Fitzherbert did not think so. She knew that Brummell disliked her and criticized her. And she dropped a hint at Carlton House that George Brummell had the impudence to laugh at them both behind their backs.

One evening at Lady Jersey's ball, Brummell took it upon himself to call the carriage of Mrs. Fitzherbert. He called out, and his voice rang out for all to hear: "Mistress Fitzherbert's carriage!" Perhaps the Prince did not hear it there and then, but it was duly reported to Carlton House.

It was also reported that Brummell had nicknamed the corpulent Regent "Big Ben" in ridicule of a most regal hall-porter at Carlton House who was called by everyone "Big Ben". The Prince was fat indeed by now, fatter and more huge than a man of fashion, or even a Prince Regent should be; and Mrs. Fitzherbert's contour was a good match—it was said that Brummell was calling them "Big Ben and Benina". Indeed, the nickname spread to all the town; from the clubs it passed into the popular puns—and the Regent was most touchy about his size.

Some little time afterwards there was a party at Claremont, in Surrey, the historic house of the Duke of Newcastle built by Vanbrugh, with domes on pillars at every corner, and two clock towers. The gardens were bedecked with statues and fountains and arches and "classic" ruins. Brummell had not received an invitation and the omission was clearly intentional, but did he not often attend parties uninvited as the Prince did from time to time? To Claremont, therefore, went Brummell in a post-chaise. But almost at the threshold he came up against "Big Ben". The Prince was extremely polite but said that the presence of Mr. Brummell was offensive to Mrs. Fitzherbert: "Unless you return to London, the party will be ruined." And he said it in a tone that Mr. Brummell had never heard before. The post-chaise reappeared at the door, and Brummell got in and departed to oblige Mrs. Fitzherbert.

It was a fatal mistake when Brummell forgot that men are ruled by women; and Mrs. Fitzherbert still possessed great influence over the Regent. Indeed her influence was all the greater because she showed a singular tact in hiding his weaknesses from the world. She even supervised his correspondence, advising him not to write to so and so: "She is careless, and leaves her papers lying about." She was even heard telling him: "Be quiet, Prince, you are drunk this evening." And Mrs. Fitzherbert was angry with Brummell, far more than he would have cared to know; the Jewish name Benina was rankling deep in her mind. Yet Brummell now discarded all reserve—threw Court etiquette and precedence of rank to the wind—he seemed bent on seeking his own destruction. (No differently did Oscar Wilde behave in the last twelve months preceding the fateful trials.) Things went round that seemed really foolish: one day, when the Prince was driving to the picture gallery in Pall Mall, Brummell was walking with a friend in the same direction; the royal carriage, so well known in St. James's because it was painted dark red and was very low, stopped at the door of the Exhibition; two sentries at the door presented arms: Brummell, who happened to pass on the pavement between the carriage and the door, with an air of grand dignity raised his hat to the salute, turning his head graciously towards the sentries and his back to the royal carriage. It was foolish, it was the joke of a naughty boy. But inside the carriage, the Prince's face was like thunder.

He said nothing, because he never knew what to say at the right moment.

Yet the Prince retaliated by repeating everywhere that "Brummell was only fit to make the reputation of a tailor"; and to Colonel MacMahon he declared: "I made him what he is, and I can unmake him as easily."

Some day Brummell called at Gray's the jewellers to inquire how his snuff-box was progressing. He was informed that the Regent had stopped the order.

It was silly and it was petty, on both sides! Brummell seemed to forget that the Prince had a revengeful nature. As Thackeray wrote of him: "The Prince Regent turned upon twenty friends, fond and familiar with them one day, and he passed them on the next without recognition."

One evening, after the Opera, the Prince, who was leaving, found his way barred by a man in a blue cloak leaning upon the check-taker's bar quite as if blocking the exit on purpose. The Prince stopped, nonplussed; the other man stood yawning at the bar. Up came a gentleman in attendance, and tapped the man in blue on the shoulder. Brummell turned his head with an air of annoyance, eyed the Prince and very slowly moved aside, raising his hat. Again, the Prince found no words for the occasion.

At the club, Brummell turned Sir Henry Mildmay and Tom Moore the poet from "Big Ben's" *coterie*: Tom Moore's defection was not so much felt, as the writer of popular romances had been unpopular at Carlton House since he had put into circulation the parody about "bringing the old King into fashion", but the defection of Mildmay was keenly felt, for Mildmay had a beautiful and accomplished wife who was quite a sensation in society.

A story went round that Brummell, after a dinner-party at Carlton House, had told the Prince: "Wales, ring the bell!" The story was not true, for Brummell, whatever his impudence, could not be so forgetful of etiquette, and the Prince was very tenacious of his dignity. The story was one of Brummell's own invention, and he used to add: "I was on such intimate terms with the Prince that if we had been alone I could without offence have asked him to ring the bell, but with a third person in the room I should never have done so—I knew him so well!"

The estrangement went on increasing. In the month of April 1812, the four leading members of Watier's, Brummell, Lord Alvanley, Sir Henry Mildmay and Henry Pierrepoint, decided to give a great ball at the Argyle Rooms. Should the Prince be invited or not? He was no longer on good terms with Brummell, and Sir Henry Mildmay was pointedly keeping away from Carlton House. Reason however prevailed: the club could not ignore and offend the Prince; moreover, it was thought by many that a gesture of deferential courtesy might help "to bring old friends together". Pierrepoint was instructed to sound Carlton House; the Prince showed alacrity at the prospect. The four despatched an invitation to the Prince in the names of all.

On the night of the ball the Prince arrived in good humour. At the door, the four dandies, candelabra in hand and wearing elegant fancy costumes, received the Prince with due ceremony. The Prince bowed to the company—his absurd bow, so incongruous with such a paunch—then he shook hands with Lord Alvanley, he shook hands with Pierrepoint and muttered some inaudible words towards Sir Henry Mildmay. Of Brummell he took no notice whatever. The insult was clear. The whole company arranged on both sides of the ballroom behind stood petrified and horrified. Then the ball went on.

When the time came for the Prince to leave, Brummell did not attend him to his carriage with his three friends.

Next day, at Carlton House, the Prince commented acidly: "Had Brummell taken the cut I gave him good humouredly, as Mildmay did, I would have renewed my intimacy with him." But would he really? And would Mrs. Fitzherbert have given her consent to it?

Some few days afterwards, Brummell was walking down Bond Street with Lord Alvanley, and suddenly they found themselves face to face with the Prince leaning, as was his affectation, on the arm of Lord Moira. The Prince stopped and talked for a few minutes with Lord Alvanley —to the ex-favourite he did not cast a glance. With his imperturbable composure Brummell greeted Lord Moira and discussed the weather. The Prince, then, moved on. Hardly had the Prince turned to go, than Brummell asked in a rather loud voice: "Alvanley, who is your fat friend?" After this there could be no question of reconciliation.

The cause of Brummell's fall from the Regent's grace was far deeper than all the current episodes. The old man in the fireless room at Caen knew only too well that the story of "Wales, ring the bell!" was apocryphal. The thing, if true, even for the winning of a bet, would be vulgar. George Brummell was often impertinent, but never vulgar.

The real cause of his fall was the same reason that caused Petronius's fall from Nero's predilection: the *Arbiter Elegantiarum* had allowed his satire to wound the Emperor, to show him up as a ridiculous poetaster and songster, worse still, as a man of rather vulgar taste, and this neither Nero nor the Prince Regent could forgive.

Brummell was to the Prince what Petronius had been to Nero. The Emperor liked Petronius immensely, but was jealous of his supreme elegance and the wit that he could not equal. The Prince Regent, notwithstanding his self-given title of "First Gentleman of Europe", was a gross person. Brummell was elegant and refined, and a wit. When the Prince thought he could destroy Brummell by childishly ignoring the Beau who had been his "model", Brummell lashed the Prince with a quip: "Who is your fat friend?" So did Petronius destroy Nero as a poet and man of fashion in a few lines of his *Satyricon*. At the height of his success, Brummell felt that he was now unassailable, that he could dare anything; and he cast the darts of his witticism against the Prince and against Mrs. Fitzherbert. Even if the Prince could have swallowed the pill, the ladies of his harem urged him to action. The Regent saw with bitterness a half-ruined Dandy disputing authority with himself, the First Gentleman of Europe. The incident of the Watier's Ball had been the material- ization of his displeasure. As a founder of the club, Brum- mell was pleased to be the host of the Prince from Carl- ton House, whom now he seldom saw there. But the Prince forgot that he was the First Gentleman.

At the Watier's Ball the Prince demeaned himself. He did not even remember the duties which hospitality im- poses upon those who have accepted it. Brummell, who had intended to oppose Dandyism with Dandyism, met the sulky attitude of the Prince with that air of elegant indifference which was his armour—but he had felt the blow.

Now there was his revenge, that terrible repartee in Bond Street: "Who is your fat friend?" And this was the one thing that the Prince, no longer handsome, no longer Apollonion, could not stand at any price; to be reminded that his figure was getting too much out of hand even for his valet. The break was final.

V

Not to be without a Court, Brummell now gave himself to the Court of the Duchess of York. He had always been a family friend of the Duchess Frederica. She was a niece of King Frederick II of Prussia, and had married the favourite son of George III. In all truth, the Duke of York was a man of utter mediocrity. At sixteen he was a Colonel in command of the English troops intended to confront Napoleon's armies in Holland and, notwithstanding defeats, he rose to the rank of Commander-in-Chief. In love with a Mrs. Clarke, he allowed the lady to sell commissions in the Army; and when the Duke refused to pay her a regular allowance, she revealed the secret of this combination. The Parliamentary inquiry showed that she had sold commissions in the Army, and as her business grew, she had also sold high offices in the Church and even the right of preaching at Court! Almost every person of position in England was involved.

The Duchess was aware of the traffic which the Duke and his mistress had carried on, but she was a person of great dignity, and her discreet behaviour was in great contrast with the society which surrounded the Prince of Wales and his undignified ducal brothers. She was also a person of excellent taste and a very nice discrimination of good breeding and manners, and the regard which the Duchess entertained for Brummell was highly creditable to him. It may, indeed, be said in favour of the manners of that day that Her Royal Highness often remarked how superior they were to the tone of those that existed at the period of her marriage, when the Duke was surrounded by a set of roués who seemed to glory in their excesses and showed a great want of refinement and courtesy in women's society.

The Duchess of York was not only a *très grande dame* in the highest acceptation of the term, but a woman of the most sound sense and judgment, with a heart full of kindness and charity. By much adroitness and tact she avoided the cabals and *tracasseries* which ruled in various branches of the Royal Family. She retained instead the constant attachment of her friends. Endowed with a superior mind, highly cultivated and well read, her conversation was full of intelligence, blended with great *naïveté*.

The Duchess lived at Oatlands among the pine-woods of Weybridge; in a rambling sort of big country-mansion, one feature of which was the number of dogs for which the Duchess had a great passion. There were some thirty dogs at Oatlands, and their comfort came before that of the visitors, who were awakened morning after morning in the early hours by their barking as they rushed along the corridors after Dawe the footman who was calling them to their breakfast. At one time there were upwards of one hundred dogs at Oatlands, and the Duchess erected monuments over the graves of her special favourites: the little monuments were grouped round a fountain in front of a grotto, to which during the summer months the Duchess used to retire with her embroidery or a book.

But the Duchess's love of animals extended in many directions. The gardens at Oatlands had an aviary in which were eagles and macaws; on the lawn monkeys played, and in the paddocks nearby could be seen kangaroos and ostriches. The company of visitors at Oatlands was excellent; but the management of the house was, probably on account of so many animals, somewhat chaotic. Mr. Charles Greville said there were stables full of horses, but never a one to ride, and a houseful of servants but never anyone to answer a bell. The Duke sat up all night playing whist, and the meals appeared at odd and unexpected moments. Still, Oatlands, because of its hostess and the sparkling wit of the guests, was one of the most agreeable houses to visit.

Brummell spent many a Christmas at Oatlands with the Duke and Duchess of York. Once his Christmas gift to the Duchess was a gown of Brussels lace which was said to have cost 150 guineas. The ceremony of presents giving was the main event at Oatlands: the great dining-room was converted into a German fair, and booths were erected round the sides, stored with various commodities. In the centre was placed a tree, the branches of which were garnished with oranges, cakes and gingerbread; on one table at the end of the room were displayed all the presents which the guests had brought to lay at the feet of the Duchess; on the other were placed the presents which Her Royal Highness presented to her friends as a keepsake. All the servants were admitted in their best attire.

There are several letters from the Duchess to Brummell, which showed the friendliness of their intercourse. One was to thank him for the present of a little dog of rare breed, which he had sent for the Duchess's fête-day.

Windsor, ce neuf de Mai.

"On ne saurait être plus sensible que je le suis au souvenir obligeant que vous avez bien voulu me donner au jour de ma fête, et au charmant cadeau que le Duc m'a remis de votre part. Recevez mes remerciments les plus sincères pour ce joli petit *chien*, c'est l'emblême de la *Fidélité*; j'aime à me flatter qu'elle sera celui de la con-

Brummell's Crest.

GEORGE BRYAN BRUMMELL

WILLIAM BRUMMELL (FATHER OF BEAU BRUMMELL)

MRS. WILLIAM BRUMMELL (MOTHER OF BEAU BRUMMELL)

GEORGE BRYAN BRUMMELL AS A BOY

VIEW DOWN REGENT STREET FROM PICCADILLY

BEAU BRUMMELL, AGED 27, AT THE HEIGHT OF HIS REIGN IN LONDON

GEORGE, PRINCE REGENT, AT BRIGHTON PAVILION

(From an engraving after a portrait by Cruikshank)

FREDERICA, DUCHESS OF YORK

CARLTON HOUSE

A CORNER OF THE GOLDEN DRAWING-ROOM

THE GREAT STAIRCASE

EXAMPLES OF THE "DIRECTOIRE" MODE AT CARLTON HOUSE

(*Drawn by C. Wild*, 1817)

(*Henry Holland, Architect*)

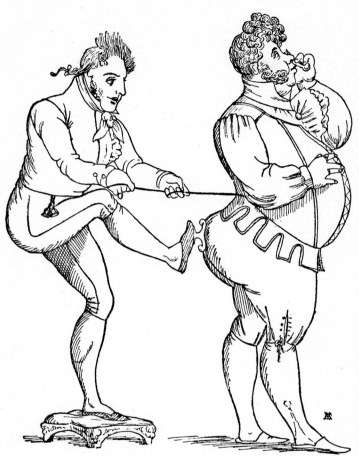

1812, OR REGENCY À LA MODE.
(*Drawn and etched by W. Heath.*)

GEORGIANA, DUCHESS OF DEVONSHIRE

(From a painting by Thomas Gainsborough in the possession of Earl Spencer)

MRS. FITZHERBERT

FRANCES, LADY JERSEY

SALON, ROYAL PAVILION, BRIGHTON

BRIGHTON PAVILION: A CONCERT IN THE MUSIC ROOM
(By Joseph Nash)

very sincerely yours

George Brummell.

BEAU BRUMMELL AT CALAIS

(From an etching in Jesse's "Life of Brummell", 1844)

THE HOUSE OF MADAME GUERIN DE SAINT-URSIN AT CAEN,
WHERE BRUMMELL LIVED FROM 1830–1832

47, RUE DES CARMES, CAEN

tinuation de notre amitié à laquelle je vous assure que j'attache le plus grand prix.

"J'ai une toux de *cimetière* qui menace ruine; si elle ne m'a pas mis sous terre avant le commencement du mois prochain, je compte me rendre à Londres, dans ce temps-là, et un des motifs qui me fait envisager avec le plus de plaisir ce séjour est qu'il me procurera l'avantage de vous y recontrer et de pouvoir vous réitérer moi-même combien je suis,

Votre toute affectionée amie et servante,

F."

There is also another letter, written to acknowledge the receipt of a note announcing the loss of a lottery ticket which they had purchased together: the paragraph alluding to the chances of his future life is happily expressed.

"I cannot say how pleased I am by the kind wishes which you have sent me for my birthday, and the charming present which the Duke forwarded to me from you. Pray accept my sincere thanks for the pretty little dog; it is an emblem of fidelity, and I am pleased to flatter myself that it will be emblematical of the nature of our friendship, upon which I place the greatest value.

"I have a racking cough, which seems likely to be the death of me, and if it has not finished me off by the beginning of next month, I hope to return to London by that time, and one of the pleasantest prospects of my stay will be the pleasure of meeting you, and of finding an opportunity to repeat that I am ever your affectionate friend and servant,

F."

Oatlands, ce 20 Septembre.

"Vous avez une manière si aimable d'annoncer les plus mauvaises nouvelles, qu'elles perdent par là de leur désagréments; je ne puis cependant que m'affliger avec vous de la perte de tous nos beaux projets de fête, qui

E 129

s'évanouissent avec la perte de notre billet de lotérie, dont je vous acquitte la dette ci-joint, et y joignent les voeux les plus sincères que ceci puisse être le dernier mauvais tour que la Fortune puisse vous jouer, et que dans toutes les autres circonstances de votre vie, elle puisse toujours vous être favorable. Ce sera me rendre justice que de vous persuader que personne ne peut s'interesser plus sincèrement à votre bonheur et à tout ce qui vous concerne.

"Je n'ai rien à vous dire de ma solitude qui puisse exciter votre curiosité, n'y ayant vu personne *de ceux qui vous* intéressent depuis votre depart. J'espère que vous reviendrez bientôt dans ces contrées, et qu'il me sera permis de vous réitérer moi-meme ici les assurances de l'amitié sincère et de la considération parfaite avec laquelle je suis,

Votre toute affectionée amie et servante,

F."

"You announce your bad news so gracefully that it loses all its unpleasantness," she writes from the country. "However, I cannot but share your regret at the loss of all our proposed festivities, which have disappeared with the loss of our lottery ticket; I send my share in this herewith, and I hope most sincerely with you that it may be Fortune's last ill turn to us, and that in every other circumstance of your life she may always be favourable to you. In justice to myself, you may be persuaded that no one can be more sincerely interested in your happiness and in all that concerns you.

"I have no news to give you of my solitude that may excite your curiosity, as I have seen no-one of interest to you since you left. I hope that you will soon return to this country and it will be possible for me to express to you in person my assurance of my friendship and the sincerity with which I sign myself your very affectionate friend and servant,

F."

VI

In January of 1814 the Thames froze. It was a fantastic spectacle; the floating masses of ice having been stopped by London Bridge, now assumed a solid surface over the river from Blackfriars Bridge to some distance below Three Crane Stairs at the bottom of Queen Street, Cheapside. By the 2nd of February the Thames was a complete "Frost Fair", with a Grand Mall, named "The City Road", lined on both sides with booths and stalls. Amusements were held on the frozen river, "Lapland Mutton" was roasted and sold on the ice-fair.

But at the end of March much greater news excited London: the fall of Napoleon. On the 11th April a Treaty between the Allied Powers and Napoleon was signed. It was Easter Monday, and London was given a grand illumination, much greater than the illuminations which, from time to time had punctuated the victories in that long combat that had been the wars against France. It was the illumination for Peace, welcomed by all with thankful hearts; Carlton House had its pillars entwined with lamps; the statue of King Charles I was covered with laurels. Louis XVIII, *le désiré*, was laid up with gout at Hartwell in Buckinghamshire, and did not hurry himself to enter into his kingdom across the water; but on the 20th of April he had to face a public reception in London: the Prince Regent with many of the nobility met him at Stanmore; his postillions were clad in white, with white hats and white cockades. This fancy for exhibiting white in honour of the white Bourbon flag, took odd expressions, for some people hung from their windows sheets and pillows. Louis XVIII entered London by Kilburn, traversed in procession Hyde Park, and down Piccadilly, and by Albemarle Street went to Grillons Hotel. Here the new King of France, leaning on the arm of the Regent, hobbled into a drawing-room and sank, exhausted, into an arm-chair. The next day, at Carlton House, he was made a Knight of the Garter; then he held a levee at Grillon's Hotel, and on the morning of the 23rd left London for Dover, to embark for France. On this day, 23rd of April, the war between England and France was officially ended.

On the 1st of May the Marquis of Wellington was created a Duke, and in the same month the House of Commons granted him an annuity of £10,000 in addition to the other grants already bestowed.

There was Peace, the panacea for all evils. During all that year, and the successive year, London saw an incessant flow of foreign visitors and troops returning home from the long war. The Regent was more than ever deep in debt; in 1787 his debts had been £161,020; in 1795 they had amounted to £640,000; from 1812 to May 1815 there was paid for his debts in various amounts the sum of £341,000; and in May 1815 there remained still unpaid £339,000. But what was such a grand total of £1,480,600 of royal debts when the Regent could, in all splendour, celebrate the victory of Waterloo? On the 4th of August, from the *Bellerophon* at sea, Napoleon was sending his formal and futile protest; the Regent was severely remarked on for his conduct to his illustrious captive; but the epic was closed and there only remained to write the last canto of St. Helena. And neither London nor Europe cared.

The English troops had come back from Spain: after

Waterloo, Wellington and his lieutenants, Lord Anglesey, Lord Raglan, Sir Hussey Vivian, were followed by Blücher with the Prussian and Hanoverian Commanders. London was swarming with foreign uniforms, gigantic plumes, colossal busbys, shakos and képis of every kind.

All these troops and foreigners had their pockets full of money. There were balls, festivals, entertainments in the houses, at Almack's, in the clubs. Every evening, before dinner, there was a promenade in Hyde Park where the people could point out the Regent on horseback in great pomp, escorted by the most handsome and musical Sir Benjamin Bloomfield, his new favourite, and Lord Sefton, hunchbacked but regarded as the most exquisite of Dandies; and there were the Ladies Molyneux and Wellington, most cheered, and old Blücher, unpolished of manners but the object of wild enthusiasm; and there was Lady Mountjoy, the Duchess of Rutland, in her coach with her lackeys powdered and looking like archbishops. The cows and deer ran amid the trees of the park and the streams crossed the grass and lawns. It was a great and almost romantic sight.

At night there was furious gambling. Gay and gallant Guardsmen, tired of roughing it at the front on a beefsteak and a bottle of port, lost no time in making love as ardently as they had made war, and in losing their back pay that had accumulated thanks to a "disease" under which the army, especially the army in Spain, had severely suffered, "an affection of the military chest".

Elder brothers, who, for sake of posterity, had not gone to the war, were laid under contribution and all these levies found their way to the green-cloth tables. Some of the St. James's Clubs, whose list of members included most of the noble names of England, were now like White's, political clubs, but play was carried on in them to an extent which made many ravages in large family fortunes. General Scott, father-in-law of George Canning and the Duke of Portland, was known to have won at White's £200,000 thanks to his sobriety and knowledge of the game of whist: but the General possessed a great advantage over his partners, for he confined himself to dining off boiled-chicken with toast and water. On such a diet he could sit at the green-table with a clear head.

At Brooks's the play was of a more gambling character; Faro and Macao were played for high stakes throughout the night; Lord Robert Spencer contrived to lose the last shilling of his considerable fortune, given him by his brother, the Duke of Marlborough; General Fitzpatrick was in the same condition and the two agreed to raise a sum of money to keep a Faro bank: Lord Spencer bagged £100,000 and retired and never gambled again. George Harley Drummond, of the famous Banking House in Charing Cross, once lost £20,000 to Brummell, and it was the only time the banker had played in his life. And at Watier's the game, Macao, went on even more furiously. After a long night of hard play, the losers found themselves at the establishment of "Howard and Gibbs", most fashionable moneylenders, signing complicated deeds of "annuities".

Meanwhile what was Brummell doing? Still smarting under the break with the Regent, he was careful to put in appearance everywhere; he strolled down King Street to Almack's talking to the Duke of Wellington, the hero of the season; and the Duke was fond of Brummell, for he was big enough a man to appreciate that Brummell had won his victories in the drawing-rooms of London, and it was as hard a battlefield as any!

But a certain decline was taking place in Brummell. As

long as he lived in the entourage of Carlton House, he had made so good and judicious a use of his income that he succeeded in posing as a wealthy man, appearing much wealthier than he really was, and he had maintained his place among the greatest names of the kingdom, all certainly much wealthier than himself. He did not go to the clubs to bet or to gamble; and on the occasion when he had a game of cards, fortune was on his side and he usually won. It was said that at one time or another he had won big sums.

But after the break with the Regent and the return of the officers from the war, he succumbed to the general inclination, and took to gambling heavily. He lost, and the more he lost the more he gambled in the vain hope of recouping his losses.

The man in the mean room at Caen knew it only too well that the "decline and fall" was not actually caused by the quarrel with the Prince. It was caused by a much more simple and dreadful reason, lack of funds. A man of fashion should always be a duke, or have the income of a duke. George Brummell did not possess inexhaustible means, and when his own fair, but utterly insufficient funds came to an end, the decline set in—to be followed by the inevitable fall.

A man of fashion, a truly elegant man such as George Brummell was, should be spared the worries of monetary embarrassment. One cannot be always exquisite in manners if one must contemplate a mundane outlook. One shrinks, at first, from approaching a friend—"to touch him", such a distasteful thing for both parties! One borrows, at first it seems easy, one is inclined to forget that some day one will have to repay the money one spends so easily. Then, one must learn the "art of borrowing": and it is not an easy art. One makes slips, shuddering at first, later on with a mere shrug—one must live somehow!

And the fall awaits round the corner. That's all. And one is no longer a man of fashion.

The handsome sum of £20,000 which he had won from the banker Drummond, Brummell lost at White's in five nights. He cried aloud: "I have lost my last shilling! I wish someone would bind me never to play again!" His friend Pemberton Mills, who was standing by, angrily watching his dear friend persist in such madness, called up: "I will." Mills handed Brummell a ten-pound note, and said: "You will forfeit a thousand if you play again at White's within a month." Brummell took it and walked out with his friend. But in a few nights he was there again, losing heavily. His friend Mills tapped him on the shoulder: "Now you should forfeit a thousand, but at least you should give me back the ten pounds."

Everything he did at the tables went wrong. At that time he lost a silver sixpence with a hole in it, which had been given him, years before, by a gipsy with the injunction that he should take care of it for everything would go well with him as long as he had it. In an evil hour, by mistake, Brummell gave the sixpence to a hackney coachman. Frantically he advertised for it—but never found it again.

He changed his residence, in a half-hearted attempt to economize, superstitiously hoping that it might change his luck. From the imposing house in South Street he moved to No. 13 Chapel Street. It was a more modest residence, a house belonging to a certain Hart, steward to the Duke of Gloucester. It was next to a mews, rather distasteful for the Beau who, in former times, had objected to country gentlemen at the club, "redolent of stables and bad blacking". The house in Chapel Street had a drawing-room and a back-sitting-room and, of course, a dining-room. Brummell, who had quietly sold some of his best Buhl furniture, moved to Chapel Street many beautiful pieces, and the artistic objects that were, like his friends, part of his very life. There was, in the dining-room, the fine silver and cutlery, and the Sèvres dinner-service, and the fine wine-coolers, and the silver tea-kettle embossed and chased in the fashion of the day, for he must still contrive to give occasional dinner-parties, although he had dispensed with his cook, the man who for years had made his dinners a social event. In his dressing-room there was the delightful wash-basin and ewer, in gold china and mazarine blue, the ewer with a silver handle, and the whole richly decorated with exotic birds finely painted in compartments, each with the name lettered in. There was still, of course, his cheval-glass, with ormolu arms for candles and in his new drawing-room there was his chintz-covered furniture and a good Brussels carpet. On the walls hung portraits of the old King, and of Lord North, benefactor of the Brummells; and the portrait of Nelson and Pitt, and one of his own friend the young Duke of Rutland. There were prints by Cipriani and Bartolozzi, and the back-sitting-room formed the library and studio. The books not too scholarly, they were the books of a worldly man of good taste in reading as in everything else. Some good historical works, the standard Poets, two editions of Shakespeare, his friend Ellis's *Specimens of Early English Metrical Romances*, bound in curiously raised calf; the *Memoirs of de Grammont*, Berrington's *Abelard and Eloisa*, a collection of novels, all beautifully bound.

Losses at cards always go hand-in-hand with debts— and debts, in turn, involve moneylenders. Occasionally, Brummell had recourse to moneylenders before the period of his downfall—and so had his intimate noble friends. There was almost a comforting pleasure in thinking that Lord Robert Manners and Lord Alvanley had thought it quite proper to make debts together with their friend Brummell. One wonders, who had gone to discuss the deal with the moneylenders? Were the deals signed and delivered at Brummell's rooms? Even more one is left wondering at the lack of business sagacity in Brummell, no less than in his noble friends.

Some years ago at Belvoir Castle, the home of the Duke of Rutland, some papers and manuscripts came to light in the muniment room, and among these papers a number of covenants were found, made jointly by George Brummell and Lord Robert Manners to pay annuities in return for sums received. There is one dated the 29th May 1811, covenanted between George Bryan Brummell, Esq. and Lord Robert Manners to pay an annuity of £100 to William Walker of South Lambeth, in return for the sum of £600 to be paid by the said William Walker to George Brummell and Lord Robert Manners. Another is similar, the annuity being £180 against a capital sum paid to Brummell and Lord Manners of £1,080. There is another paper dated three years later, signed only by Lord Charles Manners. In all there are six documents, the total sum handed by the annuitants to Brummell and Lord Manners being £4,816, and the amount to be paid annually during the joint lives of Brummell and the Lords Robert and Charles Manners being £744. Considering that in 1811 Brummell and Lord Robert were about thirty-three years old and in 1814 Lord Charles was about the same age, in less than seven years they would have paid back the whole sum and be indebted to pay over a thousand pounds a year for the rest of their lives!

Lord Alvanley had, at that time, the knack of disappearing periodically across the water, whenever he felt it was prudent to withdraw from the too greedy hands of a tenacious creditor. Brummell could still manage to spurn a creditor with an impertinent pun. One day, in a crowded room at White's one of his creditors felt he could openly ask Brummell for the return of a loan. He was a young *nouveau riche* who had longed for election to the club, and had gained Brummell's support with the loan of a thousand guineas. Brummell thought the request of repayment in detestable taste, and without moving a muscle, replied: "I thought I had repaid it." The other fellow opened his eyes wide: "When?" "You ask when? Why, the day before yesterday, when I was at the window, and saw you passing in the street, and I said: 'Good-day Jimmy, how are you?'" It was witty, it was impudent, it was in Brummell style; but it was unwise, and it lowered his prestige. To be in debt was one thing; to avow that he had taken a "loan" in payment for sponsoring a *nouveau riche*'s entry into a fashionable club was a different thing altogether; worse still, it was indelicate.

The climax came in May 1816. The best version, and the bitterest, as the old gentleman of Caen learnt with a deep frown when he had read it in after years!—is the version given by Harriette Wilson, the courtesan, in her *Memoirs*. (Harriette Wilson, the old gentleman thought, had always hated him—she had been jealous of George Brummell in the days of his glory, that's what she was, the cunning bitch, jealous of him!) She says in her *Memoirs:*

"Brummell, Alvanley and Worcester agreed to raise thirty thousand pounds, on their joint securities. Brummell, having made Worcester believe that he was, at least, competent to pay the interest of the debt, the money was raised, and the weight of the debt was expected to fall on the Duke of Beaufort, who, after strict inquiry, partly ascertained that Brummell was deeply involved, and without even the most remote prospect of ever possessing a single guinea. When Meyler heard this, he became furious, both on his friend Worcester's account, and his own, declaring that Brummell had borrowed seven thousand pounds from him, which he had lent, in the fullest conviction that Brummell was a man of honour.

"I asked Meyler how he could be so very stupid as to have been deceived, even for an instant, about Brummell? 'Why, did not everybody think so?' 'Certainly not. Brummell was pretty generally known for a man destitute of feeling, or principle; but he looked well, at an assembly, and was the fashion.' 'I would forgive him the seven thousand pounds he has robbed me of; but, on Worcester's account, I shall expose him tomorrow at White's!' 'Why not let Worcester fight his own battles?' 'That's just what, for the Duchess of Beaufort's sake, I wish to prevent.' 'I think you may trust Worcester, who has no sort of inclination to fight Brummell, nor anybody else.' 'No matter. Brummell I will certainly expose; because he has basely obtained a sum of money from my friend.' 'So has Lord Alvanley.' 'But then Lord Alvanley may, at least, contrive to pay the interest; therefore it was not so complete a fraud. Nevertheless, I hold it my duty, as an independent gentleman, never to give my countenance, nor society, to a man who has done a dishonourable action. I shall, therefore, cut Lord Alvanley wherever I meet him, notwithstanding no man delights more in his amusing qualities, than I do; but believing that society would be so much improved, by general firmness of this kind, no power on earth should prevail on me to swerve from this, my fixed determination.'

"Meyler strictly adhered to this resolution, to the day of his death. Even when he met Lord Alvanley, in the Duchess of Beaufort's box, or no matter where, he never spoke to him again. Alvanley used to rail at Meyler for this, as might, naturally, be expected, calling him a d——d methodistical grocer, etc. The little sugar-baker kept his promise of exposing Mr. Brummell, at White's Club, where he placed himself, the following morning, for the sole purpose of saying to every man, who entered, that Mr. Brummell's late conduct, both towards the Marquis of Worcester and himself, had been such as rendered him a disgrace to society, and most unfit to remain a member of that club. Tom Raikes, I believe it was, who acquainted Brummell the next day, of this glowing panegyric on his character.

"Brummell addressed a few lines to Meyler, begging to be informed if such had, really and truly been the expressions made use of. Meyler answered that, not only had he used the expression, but, that he further proposed to return to the club, on the following day, for the sole purpose of repeating them, between the hours of two and four, to anybody who might happen to be present, and, if Mr. Brummell had anything to say to him in return, he would be sure to find him at White's during that particular time."

Brummell never made his appearance in London after the receipt of this letter, which gained Meyler the nicknamed of the Dandy-killer. Yes, poor Meyler got for his pains in exposing Brummell the nickname of "Dick the Dandy-killer". We have the confirmation of Byron for this. And in those days, the spring of 1816, Brummell was thinking: Oh, if he could only go like Byron, who in April had set forth to Ostend, complete with his carriage and servants and leaving no liabilities behind but women! Byron —who still spoke with admiration and envy of Brummell: "There are but three great men in the nineteenth century, Brummell, Napoleon and myself." But since the loss of the sixpenny piece with a hole in it, a cloud had hung over Brummell's fame as well as his fortunes; the prestige of his name was going, his fiat was no longer regarded; public events had eclipsed him, and the ladies of the *beau-monde* were far more interested in hero-worship, or in procuring a hair from the tail of Platoff's horse, than securing the good opinion of the once all-powerful Prince of Fashions.

In May he decided to go. He prepared for his flight— for a flight it had to be!—with his habitual composure and deliberation, making sure of the success and the effect as he had once studied the effect and the success of his famous cravat. Some of his friends, perhaps guessing, lent a friendly hand, though their resources were, alas, at low ebb as well. Some of the beautiful things were quietly packed—the silver, some valuable and beautiful vases of Sèvres, but he left behind with much regret the famous ewer and wash-bowl in mazarine blue decorated with exotic birds; he packed instead the blue velvet album with silver corners and clasps. On the afternoon of May 16th he wrote a note to Scrope Davies:

"My dear Scrope,
Lend me two hundred pounds. The banks are shut, and all my money is in the three per cents. It shall be repaid tomorrow.

Yours, GEORGE BRUMMELL."

Davies sent this immediate reply:

"My dear George,
It's unfortunate, but all my money is in the three per cents.

Yours, S. DAVIES."

The reply was not precisely charitable, but it was pert —in Brummell's style. And the Beau read it with a cynical smile. He then dressed carefully, with his familiar blue coat, black trousers and white waistcoat and striped stockings, looked at himself for the last time in the cheval-glass in his dressing-room, and sat down to dinner and dined off a cold fowl sent in by Watier's, and a bottle of his own famous claret. The service and the Sèvres were as perfect as ever.

Then he put on his cloak, his opera-hat, and by a hack-ney carriage he went to the Opera. A noble friend had already arranged for a post-chaise to stand ready for him, near the theatre door. He sat idly at the Opera in his box, nodding at friends and ladies on right and left, suave, charming, amusing, his usual self, turning his steady and cynical eyes upon the brilliant scene he would never see again. He left early; stepped into the chaise, and vanished. At an agreed point he joined his own carriage, loaded with the few belongings he was taking with him; and as fast as post-horses could carry him, drove through the night to Dover.

Before dawn he was aboard a vessel, and made sail for the coast of France. Some hours later George Brummell disembarked at Calais. He was thirty-eight.

PART THREE

The Beau in Exile

I

Brummell arrived in Calais on the 17th of May, and went right away to the fashionable Hotel Dessein's. The first thing he did was to sell to the proprietor, M. Quillacq, his carriage that he had brought on the ship with him: from that moment he did not anticipate further use for a post-chaise.

Calais was, at that time, a sanctuary of English debtors. It was teeming with fashionable and not so fashionable gentlemen who found it most convenient to shake off the dust of England on the ramparts of Calais. At Dessein's —described by Thackeray and drawn by Rowlandson— Brummell was served with the same *fricassée* of chicken which the Reverend Sterne, travelling in the *désobligeante* lined with green taffeta, had recorded in his *Sentimental Journey*. The following day, with much tact, he wrote a letter to his two great friends, the Lords Charles and Robert Manners:

Calais, May 18, 1816.

"Dear Lords Charles and Robert,

"Persecuted to the worst extent by those to whom I was indebted, without resource or even the hope to evade or protract the execution of those menaces which, I was well assured, would have been instantly enforced against my personal liberty, I have been driven to the only alternative yet left me upon earth—that of quitting my country for ever. I am indeed most sensible, most acutely so, of the heavy wrongs which such a step must inflict upon those who from their former friendly regard for me were in-

147

duced to impose themselves a future charge for my immediate assistance. I will not endeavour to palliate the past or the present—such an endeavour would be vain and only justly prove an aggravation of my misconduct. I have no extenuation to advance beyond the desire to retain the only blessing, if such it can be called, still within my reach, which is personal freedom and even that I would have voluntarily yielded could I have felt assured its surrender might in any way have exonerated you from the trust in which you have been involved on my account. The responsibility would still have existed the same on your parts had I forfeited myself to a gaol.

"In acknowledging my obligations to you, for great they are, and in lamenting my inability to repay them, I still feel anxious in the wish to realize the promised power of future remuneration. It was very far from my deliberate intention to retire to another country and encumber you with the responsibility incurred for my service without even indemnifying you from risk in the event of death, by insuring my life, but that would now have been of no avail for my departing from England would have annulled the policies. It was the pressure of circumstances which compelled me to adopt so precipitate, and I will say so disgraceful, a measure at the exigence of the moment.

"The last remaining hope of my broken fortunes consists in a considerable sum of money now vested in the Court of Chancery which must ultimately become mine. This reversion I abandon legally and willingly to you. It is the last proof of honourable feeling I can leave in your hands to show that, although unfortunate and inconsiderate, I am not destitute of strong feeling and gratitude towards those who have been so seriously my friends.

"Whatever construction you may place upon my past conduct I trust you will do me the justice to believe that in this last act of restitution I deprive myself of every worldly support, I abandon my country a beggar and I can look forward to no means of subsistence beyond the year—yet I feel some remote satisfaction in the idea that the slight reparation I am offering is everything that is left to your former friend

GEORGE BRUMMELL."

It was most proper that he should so write to the two friends who were co-signatories with him of the fatal annuities, and which their wealthy father, the Duke of Rutland, would have no alternative but to buy up. Four days later he wrote to his friend Thomas Raikes, and it was clear from this letter that he was taking his exile with good calm and poise.

Calais, May 22, 1816.

"Here I am restant for the present, and God knows solitary enough in my existence. Of that, however, I should not complain, for I can always employ resources within myself, was there not a worm that will not sleep, called conscience, which all my endeavours to distract, all the strength of coffee, with which I constantly fumigate my unhappy brains, and all the native gaiety of the fellow who brings it to me, cannot lull to indifference beyond the moment; but I will not trouble you upon that subject.

"You would be surprised to find the sudden change and transfiguration which one week has accomplished in my life and *propria persona*. I am punctually off the pillow at half-past seven in the morning. My first object—melancholy, indeed, it may be in its nature—is to walk to the pier-head and take my distant look at England. This you may call weakness; but I am not yet sufficiently master of those feelings which may be called indigenous to resist the impulse.

149

"The rest of my day is filled with strolling an hour or two round the ramparts of this dismal town, in reading, and the study of that language which must hereafter be my own, for never more shall I set foot in my own country. I dine at five, and my evenings have as yet been occupied in writing letters.

"The English I have seen here—and many of them known to me—I have cautiously avoided; and with the exception of Sir W. Bellingham and Lord Blessington, who have departed, I have not exhanged a word. Prince Esterhazy was here yesterday, and came into my room unexpectedly without my knowing he was here. He had the good nature to convey several letters for me upon his return to London. So much for my life hitherto on this side of the water.

"As to the alteration in my looks, you will laugh when I tell you your own head of hair is but a scanty possession in comparison with that which now crowns my pristine baldness; a convenient, comely scalp, that has divested me of my former respectability of appearance (for what right have I now to such an outward sign?) and if the care and distress of mind which I have lately undergone had not impressed more ravages haggard and lean than my years might justify upon my unfortunate phiz, I should certainly pass at a little distance for *five-and-twenty*."

He had been the King of Fashion—he knew that exiled kings never return. They leave behind only a regret. Soon the echo reached him of the sale of his things at Chapel Street. The sale was ordered by the Sheriffs of Middlesex at the pressing request of Brummell's creditors, and James Christie, the Auctioneer, prepared and advertised the sale, which took place only five days after Brummell's flight, on the 22nd of May. The catalogue was a delight.

A Catalogue
of
A very choice and valuable assemblage
of
Specimens of the rare old Sèvres Porcelaine,
Articles of Buhl Manufacture,
Curiously Chased Plate,
Library of Books,
Chiefly of French, Italian and English Literature, the best
Editions, and in fine condition.
The admired Drawing of the Refractory School Boy, and
others, exquisitely finished by Holmes, Christall,
de Windt, and Stephanoff.
Three capital double-barrelled Fowling Pieces,
By Manton.
Ten dozen of capital Old Port, sixteen dozen of Claret
(Beauvais), Burgundy, Claret and Still Champagne,
The whole of which have been nine years in bottle in the
Cellar of the Proprietor;
Also, an
Assortment of Table and other Linen, and some
Articles of neat Furniture;
The genuine property of
A MAN OF FASHION,
Gone to the Continent;
Which,
By order of the Sheriff of Middlesex!
Will be sold by Auction
By Mr. Christie,
On the premises, No. 13 Chapel Street, Park Lane,
On Wednesday, May 22nd, and the following day.

On reading this catalogue, Brummell had thought of
his drawing-room which had a chimney-glass in a carved

ebony frame, chintz furniture and a Brussels carpet; the back drawing-room had also a chimney-glass, book-shelves, and library bookcase. And his dinner-service had consisted of twelve oval dishes, twenty soup-plates, seventy-eight meat-plates, nine wine-coolers; there was a breakfast-service for eight persons, three claret jugs, twelve hock glasses, forty wine glasses, decanters, etc. There were sixteen pairs of sheets, forty huckaback towels, and napkins. And he thought of the superb pair of oval Sèvres vases, which the newspaper said had sold for nine-teen guineas: they were green, with flowers and fruit, and mouldings of burnished gold. The small cup and cover of the same Sèvres china had fetched eighteen pounds; but his famous ewer and basin, mazarine-blue-and-gold ground, richly ornamented with birds and exotics finely painted in compartments, with the name of each speci-men upon them, the ewer with a handle of silver, had only fetched twenty-six pounds. He almost felt a prick of pride in reading that his silver tea-kettle, embossed and chased, had reached the price of forty-seven pounds. The set of prints, "A Family Party Dinner", fetched eighty-five guineas. It was natural that a crowd of fashionable people should have attended the sale and the papers mentioned Lord Bessborough, Lord Yarmouth, Lady Warburton, Sir W. Burgoyne, General Phipps, Mr. Mills. The Duke of York was not there in person, but had given orders for some Sèvres china to be bought for him. He wondered who had bought his letter-scale made as a Cupid weighing a heart with a brace of doves, in ormolu on a black marble plinth. The Beauvais claret, for which the Beau's table had been famous, sold for five pounds eight shillings the dozen bottles; the champagne, three pounds five shillings; the port, four pounds five shillings. Well, somebody was going to enjoy his cellar! Ah, someone had wondered why there were only six silver spoons and four forks? Alas, they had to be left behind as they had been used for his last meal!

The sale, the papers said, had realized eleven hundred pounds; but it was quite clear that Brummell had managed to get away some of his most cherished things. The competition among the buyers for knick-knacks and *objets-de-vertu* had been very keen, everyone apparently keen in securing a personal memento. When Mr. Christie had put up a very handsome snuff-box, on opening it it was found to contain a piece of paper with these words: "This snuff-box was intended for the Prince Regent, if he had conducted himself with more propriety towards me." It was the Parthian shaft!

After some two or three months at Dessein's, Brummell felt he would like to be again *chez-soi* in an apartment; and looking round in Calais, he found in the Rue Royale, just off the Place d'Armes, in a house which had formerly been the Hotel d'Angleterre, a bookseller's shop at the sign of *Le Pauvre Diable*.

The name, he felt, was suited to the circumstances; Brummell went in, and met Monsieur Leleux. M. Leleux was definitely a character. From the moment he raised his odd cap with a snipe-bill peak to his visitor who gravely responded raising his Lock's hat, Brummell saw that M. Leleux, the best bookseller of Calais, was definitely a character. They chatted of books and of travels, Leleux putting his visitor at ease with his excellent English. Leleux had a military bearing. He had acquired it, he said, in the Garde Nationale. So had his visitor been an officer; but no, he had not served during the wars. Leleux revealed, instead, that he had been in the tent of Francisco Miranda, the Dictator of Venezuela. From the life of the camp he had now retired to the peaceful and philosophical life of a bookseller in quiet Calais. And he proffered his box of snuff. "Would M. Leleux taste a pinch of his own personal mixture?" And Brummell opened, with his inimitable flick of the left thumb, his own beautiful box. And he mentioned what was in his mind: "Could M. Leleux suggest and recommend him a good lodging? He was still at Dessein's, quite comfortable, but not as comfortable as it might be in his own apartment and rooms. . . ."

"Nothing could be simpler," answered the old soldier of venture; he himself had, above the shop, some very convenient rooms. And they ascended together the staircase to the first floor. Leleux opened the doors: "This could be a drawing-room, this one, which is adjoining, would make a good dining-room; they are both front rooms; the one on the other side of the passage could be a most convenient bedroom."

Brummell liked the rooms, and even more he liked the landlord. They were to remain friends for fourteen years. Many years afterwards, M. Leleux used to speak with admiration of his former tenant: "Le pauvre monsieur était si amusant, qu'on ne pouvait rien lui refuser! Sir, I would have kept him for nothing if he would have stayed; ah, he certainly was a very droll fellow!"

No sooner was Brummell in possession of the rooms than he set about furnishing them in the most elegant and expensive manner. He had not much money, alas, but he was certainly going to re-create the atmosphere of Chesterfield Street (of the house in South Street he preferred not to think for it was a memory that he would rather sponge away from his mind).

He went therefore to a banker, M. Jacques Leveux, and deposited with him £1,000, that is the handsome sum of 25,000 francs. The banker had been recommended by the landlord Leleux, and Brummell found the name quite acceptable. There was indeed a kind of whimsicality in having henceforth his existence divided and distributed between Leleux and Leveux. (And also the banker Leveux would, in after years, say like the landlord Leleux: "One could refuse him nothing; he was simply a seductive person!")

Leleux and Leveux introduced him to a courier, and this man of business ordered and purchased for him all the furniture he required for his *salon* and his bed-chamber. Even in exile Brummell retained his taste for the resplendent Buhl furniture, heavy, massive and colourful; and it was a most pleasant diversion to furnish the three rooms in the elegant and costly style of Louis Quatorze. Sometimes a delightful cabinet did not fit pleasantly enough, and it had to be sent back to Paris and disposed of, of course at a little loss; but the courier took on himself all these troubles and worries, and his client Monsieur Brummell was a gentleman who did not bother about money, as long as the result was satisfactory. At length, after incalculable pains, and many anxious days, Brummell managed, in spite of poverty, to complete the furnishing of his three rooms in a style that could not be improved even by the most fastidious collector. In the drawing-room there was a large cabinet with doors enclosed by shining brass-wire in elegant pattern, and in this cabinet was displayed a service of Sèvres, decorated with portraits of the beauties of the Courts of Louis XIV and Louis XV; the visitors called it Brummell's harem in a Buhl *seraglio*. Brummell was so enchanted and proud of those beauties painted on Sèvres that he used to inform his visitors that it was "almost profanation even to look at these frail fair ones".

The walls of this room were covered with pictures and prints, a few of these pictures being by the brush of a young

Calais artist who Brummell decided to patronize by way of encouragement. Some books, in handsome bindings of morocco or silk, rested upon card-tables; and in the centre of the room, upon a fine Aubusson carpet, was a circular table crowded with a collection of valuable snuff-boxes, miniatures, card-cases, paperweights, little portfolios, in every variety of gold, enamel, mother-of-pearl, ivory and tortoiseshell, embossed leather and embroidered satin. Among this collection there was an ormolu greyhound, a paperweight of Siena marble topped by a small bronze eagle which had been presented to Brummell by Monsieur de Montrond, Talleyrand's secretary. At one time it had pressed the dispatches and private papers of Napoleon.

It was Brummell's most prized collection, which, like all collectors, he valued far beyond its intrinsic value; but many of these objects had been given to him by that "amiable woman", the Duchess of York. And in this room he had also installed the easy-chair the Duchess of York had presented to him, all embroidered by her hand.

Soon after being installed in the rooms he engaged a valet, called François Sélègue, commissioned a jeweller to execute for him a snuff-box of black shell and gold; and seated in his *fauteuil*, surrounded by his Buhl, paintings, prints, knick-knacks and the Sèvres portraits of La Vallière and the other beauties of the Court of France, Brummell was now ready to hold his levee once again, and brave the future.

From this point Brummell's life became like a king's exile, with all the grandeur and all the misery of a king in exile. His life—much too long—took on a hundred shades: it became pathetic, comic and tragic. But it was a unique life: the immortality of Brummell was truly achieved in those years of long and painful exile. England might have utterly forgotten him; instead, it remembered him forever. And so did the whole world.

II

It must be said that Fortune did not forsake Brummell: like a true king in exile, he was supported by his friends. His friends from London placed at his disposal sums of money, often considerable: and it was more than generosity, it was the support of a cause. Shortly after his arrival, a clerk from M. de Vos, a Calais banker, called one morning on Brummell to place a large sum in his hands—the equivalent of £1,000—which had been paid into their bank the day before; the donor wished to remain anonymous.

The old King's son-in-law, the Duke of Gloucester, during one of his frequent visits to Paris, stopped at Calais and called at *Le Pauvre Diable* "to make sure that the Beau in his solitude lacked no comfort". But in the circle of those who provided not only to his wants but to his luxuries (and they knew that only the luxuries were his real wants!) no one extended relief and help to the expatriated Brummell with more warmth of feeling or delicacy of manner than the Duchess of York. The "*votre très affectionée amie et servante*" of her witty letters sent now frequent tokens of her friendship: a purse, a card-case, a note-keeper, the work of her own fair hands; and when opened, these little marks of Her Royal Highness's regard were never found empty, and a rustling of banknotes was always heard within their folds. The kindness of this Royal Lady was the more meritorious on account of her high rank, and it proved that women are ever the most lasting in their attachment of love and friendship.

The friends, too, headed and urged by the faithful Lord Alvanley, immediately spoke at White's of clubbing together to provide Brummell with an annuity. The idea was, for the moment, left in abeyance; but many came forward: John Chamberlayne, who had never been intimate with Brummell, went so far as to announce that he would personally provide Brummell with a yearly allowance, and so began it. The Marquis of Lorne, one of the old intimate circle, although compelled to run to Paris for his own safety, stopped in Calais and left what money he could. And many others, in the course of time, sent or came to give substantial proofs of their regard: the Duke of Rutland (magnanimously forgiving the financial escapade of the Beau with his two sons); the Dukes of Richmond, Beaufort and Bedford; Lords Sefton, Jersey, Willoughby, Craven, Ward, Stuart de Rothesay. Even the Duke of Wellington—who was occasionally crossing the Channel, the gossips said, to make sure that the ghost of Napoleon was not walking about Waterloo—visited Brummell, and courteously left his token of esteem and sympathy.

That Brummell, even after his departure from London, still retained friends stands to prove the permanency of his influence. Society is only too prompt to discard and forget those who have played their brief part upon the fashionable stage. Brummell in exile was still king: it was impossible to discard a man who displayed such confidence in the kindness of his friends, and accepted their help only on condition that any attempt to relieve his anxieties should be made with due formality. There was a delightful sense of humour in his receiving and entertaining his friends in his old superb style, only the reception was always at the visitor's expense.

Also the choice of Calais had been a most diplomatic

one: hardly had Louis XVIII returned to his throne than English Society crossed the Channel to re-visit Paris, and Calais became a meeting-place between London and Paris; and in the eyes of society people the little town of Calais was now dignified by the presence of George Brummell. It became normal to make a pilgrimage to the ci-devant King of Fashion. And Brummell, born for Society and living solely for it, pursued his life in Calais with the same idle and haughty pose.

Happily for him, he had not learnt the difference between the necessities and the luxuries of life. Although he had written to Tom Raikes that he was leaving his bed at seven, actually he rose about nine o'clock. He breakfasted, *café-au-lait complet* in his brocaded dressing-gown, and sat reading *The Morning Chronicle* and some new books until noon. Soon after his arrival in Calais he commenced to learn French, and took as teacher an old abbé "who"—he wrote to Tom Raikes—"instructs me in the French dialect at three francs an hour". Scrope Davies, who liked to make fun of his friends, used to say that the Beau, in his French studies, had been "stopped, like Napoleon in Russia, by the Elements"; but in fact, Brummell came to speak and write French quite well and not without elegance.

Precisely at twelve—so precisely that Leveux's assistants kept their dinner time by it—"*Ah, voilà M. Brummell, c'est midi*"—Brummell might be seen in his flowing dressing-gown and velvet cap crossing the passage to his bedroom. His toilet then commenced, and it occupied nearly two hours: he shaved with the smallest of razors, and after shaving he plucked away all superfluous hairs with a pair of tweezers, using a dentist's magnifying glass; he washed profusely, and then dressed with the old meticulous care. Thus properly attired, he held his levee and sat *en Prince* chatting with the friends who dropped in. It was at one of those levees that one day an acquaintance burst out in an alarmed voice: "Brummell, have you heard the news? S——, the banker, ran off last night!" "Well, what of that?" "Why, I have lost a thousand francs." "Then, my dear fellow, in future take hint from me, and always keep your account overdrawn!"

At four o'clock punctually he stepped into the Rue Royale, blue coat, buff waistcoat and marvellous cravat, and proceeded for a walk on the ramparts. It was a walk *pour se montrer*, not certainly for exercise; a walk such as he would have taken down St. James's Street, on his way to the "bow-window" at White's. The "long walk", as Brummell termed it, was going in at one gate and out at the other, a distance of two hundred yards; and he would adjust his pace to that of his dog Vick, a bitch terrier, that was rather fat, and even during this short promenade Brummell was obliged to turn round and wait for Vick at least a dozen times. But Brummell loved this dog, and once when Vick was very ill, he sent for two of his friends who were competent in dogs' illnesses, and they found Vick laid up upon her master's bed, and Brummell in great distress. The two "Vets" expressed the opinion that the dog ought to be bled. "Bled!" said the master in terror, "I leave the room, call me when the operation is over." Some years later Vick died of obesity and old age; Brummell buried her in Dessein's garden, and for several days put on mourning and talked of erecting a monument to her memory. His *salon* was closed to visitors for three days, and for several weeks he did not allow anyone to speak of her death. He consoled himself with a trio of poodles, the most famous of the three was named Atout, and had been trained by a soldier of Calais garrison, and he was turned out for his walk on the ramparts as neat as Brummell. The greatest accomplishment of Atout was to take a hot muffin from the plate before the fire, and run round the room offering it to the company.

At five o'clock the Beau—and his dogs—ascended to his rooms and dressed for dinner. Dinner was at six and was sent in by Dessein's, but served by Brummell's personal valet. With the meal, when alone, he drank a bottle of Dorchester ale, of which he had a barrel in the house: the humbler drink showed that he had "fallen from his high estate"; but Dorchester ale was at least malt liquor; and this potent stuff was followed by a glass of brandy, which he always took during dinner; and the rear was brought up by a bottle of Bordeaux. He was never drunk, although he had been well accustomed to deep potations of wine, to say nothing of "Roman punch", into the mysteries of which he had initiated the Prince Regent. Only once was he seen inebriated. It was at Calais, and indeed he was so disgusted with himself that he performed a voluntary penance of solitary confinement for eight days. Dinner at six was kept as a ritual, in memory of London; once, when Lord Westmorland, passing through Calais, called on him and said he would be happy if he would dine with him at three o'clock, Brummell answered: "Your lordship is very kind, but I really could not feed at that early hour!"

At seven o'clock, or half-past, he went to the theatre, where he had a small box; or in the long summer evenings he retired to the garden of his house, in the honeysuckle-covered *berceau*, and there he read or noted down the recollections of his past and more resplendent days.

The friends that came to visit him found him as amusing as ever. Even his valet was a marvel, *bien poudré, bien cérémonieux et bien mis*. To the callers the valet would say that "Monsieur was shaving, but would receive during his second toilet".

From his friends Brummell learnt of the gradual decline of Watier's Club: the play had become so high that most of its members were ruined by it. Some had committed suicide, others had followed the example of the Beau and gone into exile. Berkeley Craven (a school-fellow at Eton!) had retired to St. Homer; Scrope Davies had gone to Paris: "Poor Davies, so witty, to reduce himself to one room in Paris! And they tell me that no one is ever allowed to penetrate in that room, but each day poor Scrope issues from it immaculate, and receives his friends in the gardens of the Tuileries."

One day that a friend glanced round the exquisite room with its expensive furniture and knick-knacks, Brummell told him: "My friend, it is a truly aristocratic feeling the gift of living happily on credit! One must, of course, be endowed with the gift of having no idea of the value of money." And to Harriette Wilson who inquired how he managed to amuse himself in Calais, the answer was: "I have never been in any place in my life where I could not amuse myself."

His drawing-room, his mode of life, his reputation, indeed his fame were the topic of all society in Calais and the neighbourhood. People sought his company; the gentlemen attended his levees, the wealthy *bourgeois* were glad to have him at their dinner-tables. But Brummell was most careful in the choice of his friends, and loftily severe with those who manifested a disposition to intrude upon him without due introduction. One day, when walking on the ramparts arm-in-arm with Lord Sefton, they met an extremely vulgar looking Englishman, who bowed to Brummell in a familiar way. "Sefton," said Brummell, "what can that fellow mean by bowing to you?" "To me!

He is bowing to you, I suppose, for I know no one in Calais." Soon after, the stranger passed them again and patting Brummell's arm confidentially, said in a most cordial tone: "Don't forget, Brumm, don't forget, goose at four!" Brummell stared after the fellow, and laughed aloud: "My dear Sefton, it is always the vulgar friend who is most profuse at the wrong moment!"

His letters to his friends were very chatty, the letters that a man who has retired to his country-seat in a fit of misanthropy would write to his friends in town:

"Dear Hughes,

"*Rob Roy* arrived here in a storm more bleak than those which usually dwell upon his native hills; I had received and read him before, but that does not in the least diminish my obligation to your good-natured memory—a thousand thanks to you for sending him.

"I rejoice in the re-establishment of Devonshire's legitimacy. I had indeed been looking out for an economical two-pair of stairs retreat for him in the adjacent Basse-Ville; but I am more pleased with his resurrection than, I am sure, I should have been in having him for a neighbour.

"Have you read Horace Walpole's letters to Mr. Montagu? If not, I would recommend you to get them. They are much the most pleasant light reading I have had for an age. The climate of Venice I fear has sadly impaired my friend Byron's imagination, for I never waded through such a galimatias as *Beppo*—he had better confine himself to misanthropic lamentation, for he is lost the moment he attempts to cultivate "Broad Grins" like George Coleman.

Ever truly yours,

G.B."

Once Alvanley arrived from London, always good natured and affectionate but absent-minded; and informed Brummell that the Duchess of York had given him a letter but that he had accidentally burnt it. Brummell was so desolate that he could not resist writing to her and beg for another version of it.

"You have lost nothing," the Duchess replied, "in that letter which was destined for you, and which Lord Alvanley consigned to the flames; it contained only my thanks for the charming gifts which you had the goodness to send me (with which I adorned myself on the evening of my little birthday party), and my regrets that you were no longer one of us. These regrets are renewed daily, and especially the reasons which are the cause of them. Believe that nobody feels the loss of your society more than I do. I shall never forget the agreeable moments that I have owed to it, and the only thing that would compensate me would be the certitude of your happiness, for which I send the most sincere wishes, as for that which can contribute most to it."

III

When the days were uneventful, and the English boat did not unload some friends—it was always a red-letter day in the week that on which the English packet came in—Brummell beguiled the time by jotting down on paper his memories. Indeed, towards the end of 1818 there was much talk in London about the Memoirs that George Brummell was busy writing in Calais. What a book they might have been! Charles Standish told Lady Granville that he had actually seen at Belvoir a letter from Brummell to the Duke of Rutland announcing the imminent publication of his autobiography. Others reported that Brummell had actually turned the leaves of the manuscript in front of them, saying: "Here is a chapter on Carlton House, here is one on Mrs. Fitzherbert and the Regent." Also Croker, the diarist, said he had heard something about it, that Brummell was going to publish an English Journal at Calais, which will alarm some great folk; and it was said that the French Police had been asked to have a look at it. The publisher, John Murray, had offered Brummell £5,000 for the Memoirs, and people even said that the Regent had sent Brummell £6,000 to suppress them. John Murray had even thought of going over to Calais to negotiate for the book. What a pity the publisher of Lord Byron and Sir Walter Scott did not make that journey to Calais—what a loss to posterity! Another offer came to Brummell from yet another publisher, and it came at a moment when he was in dire need of money; and yet Brummell resisted the temptation.

Leleux, his landlord, urged him to accept the offer; but his tenant told him: "I promised the Duchess of York that I would never publish any notes of mine during the lifetime of the Regent or his brothers, and I am under so many obligations to her, and have such a deep respect for her generous and amiable conduct to me in our early friendship and since, that I would rather go to gaol than forfeit my word. The Duchess of York is the only link that binds me to the life that was." Some other writing he did, little occasional verses addressed to ladies of Calais; and he put hand to a book on a subject on which he was certainly the supreme authority: "Male costume—Grecian, Roman and British Costume from the Roman Invasion to 1822." But the book was never finished. He found, in that first period of his life in Calais, much enjoyment in writing letters and he was in constant communication with the Duchess of York, Lord Alvanley, John Chamberlayne, Lieut.-Col. Hughes who was now at St. Homer. To the ladies of Calais he amused himself by writing long letters interspersed with French words and expressions.

But his greatest occupation was the making of a screen for the Duchess of York. It was a big screen of six panels about five and a half feet high and twenty-four inches wide, decorated with prints. Such screens were very fashionable at the time and Byron also enjoyed making one, pasting on it cuttings of sporting prints. Brummell, who had shown a propensity for collecting cuttings, had filled his big blue velvet album with the poems given to him by his friends, or composed by himself. He now gave himself to the making of this screen with much gusto. It was to be an artistic achievement: a chronicle of the times in pictures, allegorical as well as actual, and above all, it was to be a testimonial to a friendship which no amount of patient work with scissors and paste could ever repay.

Captain Jesse, who saw the screen, was so impressed by it that he left us this description:

"The most prominent features of it are the quadrupeds, which form the centre of the upper part of each leaf; these prints are on a scale much larger than the generality of the other drawings. In the first compartment is an elephant, the second bears a hyena, the third a tiger, the fourth a camel, and the fifth a bear. The sixth has no animal upon it. Many of the drawings which cover the remaining surface of the screen are coloured: the engravings are in line, mezzotint, or lithograph, with sketches in chalk, pastel, or pencil; in fact, a specimen of every possible variety of the limner's or engraver's art, if oils be excepted, is to be found upon it. It will therefore be easily imagined, that the general effect produced by such a multitude of objects, of every colour and form, is on the first *coup d'oeil* very confused: but, on a closer inspection, the attention that has been devoted to arrangements of almost every part becomes easily discernible: each little pictorial episode, and there are hundreds, is encircled by wreaths and garlands of flowers of every description; the rose predominating, much to the credit of the paster's taste; fruit, and emblems in character with the subject to be illustrated, are also mingled with the flowers; to give an exact description of this glorious piece of fiddle-faddle, the trifling industry of a thoroughly idle man, would be both useless and tedious.

"On the first leaf, as I have before remarked, there is an elephant, under the neck of which is a full-faced portrait of Napoleon, who, in this case, is the subject to be illustrated. By introducing this animal the Beau intended to express the Emperor's power; but on the throat of the modern king-maker is a butterfly, intended to represent another of his attributes, and to neutralize his greatness.

The portrait is encircled by the neck, shoulder, and trunk of this Chouni; and the edges of the two drawings, which would otherwise have been discoverable, are concealed by other attributes, as well as by fruit and flowers, cut out and arranged with infinite pains. This plan of concealing the edges was pursued throughout with as much nicety as a sempstress would bestow on the hem of a *chemise d'homme*. Amongst these emblems, and immediately above the Emperor's head, is a mortar elevated for firing; from the mouth of it proceeds a sword, round which a serpent has entwined itself: a scythe and a flag, with the Russian eagle on it, are crossed above the sword, and the trophy is completed by laurel branches over the emblem of Time. The trumpet of Fame, and a port-fire nearly burnt out, are above the Muscovite colours. The reader can scarcely fail to see the application of these illustrations to Napoleon's history.

"Below the elephant, and in the centre of the same leaf, are grouped four coloured portraits; the one on the left hand looking outwards is General U——n, next to him are the late Marquis of Hertford and Lord Sefton, apparently in conversation; and the fourth (to me an *inconnu*) is on their right, and looking towards them. The General, who has a neckcloth large enough for three, and a rounded shirt collar on the same scale, is smelling a sprig of jessamine; a Cupid lolls on his shoulder, as much at ease as the reading Magdalen at Dresden, and is killing, not the general, but Time, with a book, probably Ovid's *Art of Love*. On the body of the gallant officer, who is thus indulging poor Cupid with a ride a pig-a-back, is pasted an unnatural and classical-looking landscape, representing a forest in the distance, with a rocky foreground; but the principal subject is a young lady, who, having thrown aside her harp, is caressing the antlers of

a wounded stag. Back to back with the General is the
late Lord Sefton, the defect in whose figure Brummell
concealed with a flower, probably with the intention of
showing that he considered his physical infirmities were
entirely overbalanced by his amiable disposition. This he
might well do, for he was one of his greatest benefactors.
Between his lordship and the Marquis is the head of a
very lovely woman, ornamented, without the slightest
necessity, by a plume of ostrich feathers. The two peers
are so placed that it is difficult to say out of whose pocket
the divinity is emerging; most likely that of the latter.
Lord Sefton is in Hessians, and wears a very peculiar hat.
My Lord of Hertford, whose whiskers look as if they were
made of leopard's skin, is dressed in a greatcoat, and car-
ries a large cane between a pair of yellow tan gloves, his
left hand being inserted like Lord Sefton's right, in his
pocket behind. His emblems are also highly appropriate
and numerous. First, and in the front, are two Cupids in
an azure cloud, one bearing the hymeneal torch, and the
other a dove, which is looking him amorously in the face.
Cupids, in every variety of position that the coryphee of
the Grand Opera could devise, float around his lordship.
They may be literally said to swarm; and judging by
their looks, each of them seems to be laden with the sweets
of a different hive, more luscious than those of Narbonne
or Hymettus. One, much larger and more saucy-looking
than the rest, is standing on his lordship's shoulder, and
rests, with folded arms, and the domesticated air of a
favourite spaniel, upon his hat. To the right is a charming
print, by Bartolozzi or Cipriani, of a young girl attended
by the everlasting Cupids; above her is a little archer
shooting at doves in a palm tree, and around are Satyrs
carrying Bacchantes and shepherdesses in their arms.
Farther on is a gentleman who sports a pair of yellow

knee-breeches, and is presenting a nest of doves to a lady in a scarlet-bodied dress. All these subjects appear to have been *appliqué* with great judgment in honour of the most noble the Marquis of Hertford. The *inconnu*, the last of the quartette, is the counterpart of a piping bullfinch, and by the emblems that surround him may perhaps have been celebrated 'fanatico per la musica'.

"The hyena in the second compartment is represented as being tamed by the Arts, Sciences, and Religion, symbols of which, mingled with the Muses and the Graces, are seen on every side. In the centre of this leaf is a coloured print, taken from a scene in the *Fille mal gardée*. There are also various drawings representing historical, mythological and rural subjects. Amongst the most striking are Telemachus relating his adventures to Calypso, Phaeton driving his car, Time his chariot; a French dragoon at bivouac preparing a fowl for the camp-kettle; a *religieuse* at her devotions; a minuet at a French fair; a gentleman and a shepherdess, whose dog has seized the skirt of her dress, and with an anxious look is endeavouring to detach her from her admirer.

"The tiger on the third leaf is surrounded by Cupids, cows, goats, etc., all, with the exception of the first, harmless and peaceful animals. On each side of the royal brute is a coloured print, representing the juvenile amusements of the Dauphin and the Duchess of d'Angoulême. In the one to the right they are playing at soldiers: she is marching in front of her brother and beating a drum, thus indicating the resolute spirit which she afterwards showed: her dog is campering before her; and her companion, who is dressed in the national colours, is carrying a flag, on which are inscribed the words *Union*, *Force*. She has evidently tempted him away from his ninepins to follow her, and these toys are seen behind him scattered on the ground. In the other print they are playing at battledore and shuttlecock, looking very happy and very merry. The ferocious tiger was well chosen to illustrate the period and the subject to which this part of the screen is devoted; for in this beast of prey are plainly personified the cruelties of the Revolution, and, in the domestic animals, the helplessness of those who suffered by its horrible excesses. The children's ignorance of the nature of the proceedings of which their flag and their tricoloured sashes were the emblems, and their utter unconsciousness of the anxiety and danger which at that very time surrounded them, and all belonging to them, as expressed by their game of battledore and shuttlecock, is truly characteristic of their years. Such happily is generally the case with children. In the midst of the dreadful hurricane in which the crew of the *Bridgewater* so nearly perished, and when not a ray of hope existed for the safety of a soul on board, where were the little children of one of the passengers, and what were they doing? Were they frightened at the unusual trembling of the ship, as she staggered under the concussions of each succeeding wave, or sobbing in their mother's arms? No; at that awful moment they were floating their little paper boats in the water that half-filled the cabins. Below these prints are many other Cupids also, but by no means so comfortable as the one on Lord Hertford's shoulder. One poor boy is standing, in a cold wretched night, at the door of a house; his torch is thrown down in the snow, and his dripping pinions are scarcely covered by a scanty red mantle. He seems to be a good illustration of the old song, 'In the Dead of the Night', and is apparently singing the insinuating line: 'I've lost my way, ma'am; do pray let me in.' Near this mischief-maker is another smoking a pipe.

"Below the camel, in the fourth compartment, is a man

in Cossack trousers; a monkey is sitting on his back, gently exciting his own epidermis; a pensive Cupid is clinging to the coat of the incognito. Near him is a gentleman with a lady in his arms; a Cupid is looking up at them, and pointing to a volume of sermons which he holds in his hand; a butterfly has alighted on the cavalier's coat, and not far off is a group of Cupids and Satyrs rushing in among bathing Nymphs. There is also a female barber.

"The bear in the fifth compartment is stimulating his appetite with a young crocodile; around him are children at play, shepherds, the Graces, Venus, and numerous insects and shells. Lower down are portraits of Charles Fox, Necker, Sheridan, the Regent Philip of Orleans, and John Kemble. Fox has a butterfly near him; Nelson, Greenwich Hospital; Sheridan, a Cupid carousing on some straw; and Kemble, a ladybird on his waistcoat. Round the arm of a man in Hessians is a green monkey holding a mask, and another monkey is between his legs. There are also likenesses of Lucien Bonaparte, the Princess Charlotte, and Duke of Cambridge when a young man; and a little piece representing an old *curé de village* trying, but in vain, to thread the needle of one of his pretty parishioners.

"Byron and Napoleon, placed opposite to each other, occupy the upper centre of the last and sixth leaf: the former is surrounded with flowers, but has a wasp on his throat. This to his *friend* was base ingratitude on the part of Brummell, for the noble lord spoke of, and would have pasted him, with more charitable feeling. Kean, as Richard, is the last print I shall notice. He is below the Emperor, and his neck is ornamented with *two hymeneal* torches laid together crosswise by a tru-lovers' knot.

"It will be seen by this imperfect description that, to understand fully the wit in the arrangement of all the groups, it is necessary that the observer should be familiar with the gossip of the day; and there is little doubt that any of Brummell's contemporaries would, with the greatest ease, recapitulate the histories attached to each, and explain to his juniors circumstances in the arrangement that to them are merely unmeaning riddles."

But the Duchess of York died on August 6th 1820, aged only fifty-four; and the screen remained as a sad memory folded in a corner of the drawing-room in the Rue Royale, a fertile subject of conversation for Brummell's privileged visitors, and to them only was it ever shown. From the time of the death of the Duchess of York, Alvanley noticed that Brummell tended to succumb to solitude and fits of melancholy.

IV

Time went slowly by. A faint touch of decay seemed to set on Brummell. A trained eye could notice the difference. Lord William Pitt Lennox, passing through Calais, invited him to dinner at Dessein's: to his great surprise, he noticed that Brummell's well-fitting clothes were a little "seedy", his boots were not so brilliant as they used to be when he lounged up Bond Street; his hat, though carefully brushed, showed symptoms of decay, and the only remnants of dandyism left were the snow-white linen and an exceptional tie.

In Calais, Brummell had found a promising young tailor, and had taught him the cut of Saville Row. The cravats came from London, frequent gifts from Tom Raikes; but now and then the parcels proved disappointing. Once Brummell had to write to Raikes: "I am persuaded you had no hand in the mutilation of the muslin that you sent to me. No, I said, he never in cold blood could have been guilty of this outrage. The fault then rests with that vandal Chapman, who, in the attempt to exculpate himself, had added a lie to the previous offence, for according to all the rules of geometry, two triangles will form a square to the end of the world, and of equal triangular proportions are the kerchiefs in question. The intention you profess of sending me some square pieces assures me you are in good humour."

In March 1820 old King George III died at Windsor and the Prince Regent became King. Would he, now that he was King, relent towards his old friend? Brummell knew the new King too well to entertain hopes that he would stretch out a hand to help the man who had been his favourite friend and was now in weary exile. He wrote to Tom Raikes:

"He is at length King. Will his past resentments still attach themselves to his crown? An indulgent amnesty of former peccadilloes should be the primary grace influencing newly throned sovereignty; at least towards those who were once distinguished by his more intimate protection. From my experience, however, of the person in question, I must doubt any favourable relaxation of those stubborn prejudices which have, during so many years, operated to the total exclusion of one of his *élèves* from the royal notice; that unfortunate—I need not particularize.

"You ask me how I am going on at Calais. Miserably! I am exposed every hour to all the turmoil and jeopardy that attended my latter days in England. I bear up as well as I can; and when the mercy and patience of my claimants are exhausted, I shall submit without resistance to bread and water and straw. I cannot decamp a second time."

Yet, he hoped against hope. He did not want to go back to London; that was out of the question, for he thought it would be impossible to recapture his former glory, and Brummell could not fit as a mere onlooker in London life. He was quite reconciled to remain away from England, to play to the end the part of the exile; but George IV, now that the power was his, could show him indulgence and gratify him with some sinecure that would relieve him of worry and adorn him, at the same time, with some kind of official position. So were his friends in England hoping for him. Lord Alvanley wrote indeed to Earl Bathurst, who had for eight years been Secretary for War and the Colonies in the Ministry of Lord Liverpool:

"I am aware that I have little right to address you on the following subject, but I trust you will forgive my doing so on the score of old family friendship. Poor Brummell has now been four years in Calais. He has lived upon what those who were intimate with him have been able to do for him. So precarious an existence, however, is hardly worth having. I have been told that you have expressed yourself kindly with regard to him. Perhaps you might be able to give him some small situation abroad, in order to relieve him from the position in which he now is. I say nothing about the circumstances that occurred previous to his departure from England. I cannot excuse them in any way. They, however, are no longer fresh in the memory of those who were not sufferers, and I know that the greatest sufferer is most desirous that something should be done for him. The Duke of York, who has been very kind to him, would gladly assist any effort in his favour. I will not trouble you more on the subject. If you can do anything for him, I am certain you will. If not, I am certain your reasons will be better than any I could give."

The following year Brummell changed his rooms. He did not wish to leave the comfortable house of *Le Pauvre Diable*, but arranged with M. Leleux for other rooms to the left of the old ones; a dining-room on the street floor, a drawing-room on the floor above, and a handsome bedroom to the rear, all accessible by a private entry and staircase. And, as usual, the first thing Brummell did was to redecorate. He laid a floor of black-and-white marble inside the private front door, something quite grandiose, that M. Leleux used to show, years afterwards, to inquirers about his former tenant; then he adorned the dining-room with a wallpaper of rich crimson. It was an expense, perhaps in excess of the sums he was receiving from his friends in England, but he liked the rooms in the Rue Royale, and, should his hope of an official job materialize, the apartment would be worthy of the situation.

V

In September of that year, 1821, George IV came to Calais on his way to visit his subjects in Hanover (the Hanoverian King of England ceased to be titular King of Hanover after the death of William IV in 1837).

When the King of England landed, the pier was crowded with curious spectators. As he stepped ashore from his barge, his hat fell from his hand; an urchin picked it up and rushing forward restored it to His Majesty: "Big Ben" put his hand in his pocket and handed the boy a handful of golden sovereigns. Louis XVIII had deputed the Duc d'Angoulème to greet George IV on his arrival on French soil, and together they went in a carriage to Dessein's Hotel where King George would be entertained.

On that morning, M. Leleux was standing at his shop-door, from where he could enjoy a good view of the royal procession on its way to the hotel, and he saw Brummell, who had gone out for his usual walk, trying to make his way across the street to the house. But the crowd was great, and he was obliged to remain on the opposite side. When the carriage approached, all hats were taken off, and when it was close to *Le Pauvre Diable*'s door M. Leleux heard the King say in a loud voice to his confidential secretary, Sir Benjamin Bloomfield: "Good God, Brummell!" The carriage went on its way, and Brummell, pale as death, entered the house by his private door and went straight up to his rooms.

In the evening there was an official dinner at Dessein's,

and Brummell lent for the occasion his valet, Sélègne, who was also a chef, and who attended to make the punch. Indeed, Brummell sent by the valet a special bottle of Maraschino to which he remembered the King was extremely partial. It had been noticed, during the afternoon, that the King was not in good humour. Was this occasioned by the encounter of the morning? Was he worried lest Brummell would make his appearance and ask for an audience? After the dinner the King requested the Mayor of Calais to lend him a snuff-box; but the Mayor did not take snuff and had no box to offer. The Chief of Police immediately presented his. The King took a pinch, which in all probability he purposely allowed to fall on the floor, and the next morning sent the Police Chief a gold box, for George IV loved to bestow small favours in a grandiose way.

In the morning everyone of the King's suite, with the exception of Sir Benjamin Bloomfield, called on Brummell, and one and all endeavoured to persuade him to request an interview with the King, now or when he should return to England. Brummell had written his name in the register at Dessein's, but he abstained from presenting himself or writing to the King. A refusal to see him, he said to all his friends, would be an indignity to which he did not choose to be exposed.

Later Benjamin Bloomfield called, but was not sent by the King. Sir Benjamin came on the errand of asking the former Beau the courtesy of some snuff for the King, and relating the occurrence of the previous night. Would Mr. Brummell oblige him and the King?

Brummell gave Sir Benjamin a box of snuff, and that night, at the theatre, when the box was proffered in due time, an exclamation followed the first pinch: "Why, sir, where did you get that snuff? There is only one person

I know who can mix snuff this way." "It is some of Mr. Brummell's, sir." Here the conversation closed.

Two days after his arrival, the King left Calais for Cassel, and he was heard to remark to Sir Arthur Paget as the carriage drove away: "I leave Calais and have not seen Brummell."

This remark, which was heard by several persons who were assembled in the yard of the hotel, was a cruel one, for it implied that the King had, in some degree, expected Brummell to make his appearance at the public levee held at the Hotel. This remark, combined with the persuasions of his friends, somewhat diminished the fear he felt of receiving a rebuff, and Brummell determined to make some approach when the King returned to Calais, although he did not intend calling without receiving some intimation that such was the King's pleasure. The civic authorities expected that on his way back to England the King would visit the Town Hall, and Brummell thought he might be able to meet the King on this occasion. On the way back George IV was much pressed for time, and hurried on board the royal yacht immediately after his arrival. Whatever the case, Brummell and the King did not meet, and George IV showed that he lacked the finest virtue of kings, magnanimity; but, alas, he was the King! The crown had long since fallen from Brummell's head.

One morning, in 1725, an English lady presented herself at the rooms in the Rue Royale and inquired *si Monsieur Brummell était visible*. François the valet, "just such a valet as one would have given the Beau in the acme of his glory, *bien poudré, bien cérémonieux et bien mis*", answered *que Monsieur se faisait la barbe*. The lady made to go and left her card: "*Pardons*," said the valet, "*mais Monsieur reçoit en ce faisant la barbe. Monsieur est à sa seconde toilette, actuellement*." And took the card in.

It was Harriette Wilson, now married to Rochfort. The former courtesan, now forty years of age, had retired to Paris, setting herself up at No. 111 Rue du Faubourg St. Honoré, and, with the help of her publisher, John Joseph Stockdale, was writing her reminiscences in many volumes, finding it extremely profitable to extract good sums of money from well-known people simply by asking them for a contribution in return for her undertaking to leave them out of her book. The sum usually asked was £200.

She was, this day, passing through Calais, and although she did not feel any friendship for Brummell, felt inclined to pay him a hasty visit, just as the horses were being put to her carriage. She found Brummell *en robe de chambre de Florence*, and thought at first glance that if one might judge from his increased *embonpoint* and freshness, his disgrace had not seriously affected him.

VI

But things were going far from rosily for Brummell. The news that there had been no meeting at all between George IV and Brummell during the King's journey passing through Calais, had made many heads shake in London. The King had been most ungenerous, all admitted it; yet, it might have helped matters a good deal if things had gone differently.

Brummell's means of subsistence became very irregular. Also, the Duke of York did not continue, at least in a regular way, the allowance that the Duchess had most kindly passed to Brummell until her death. It required all Brummell's charms to keep his creditors quiet. "Whenever any one of my creditors calls upon me, the moment he enters the room I commence an amusing conversation. This has hitherto succeeded very well, but my stock-in-trade is drying up!"

Yes, he could be very whimsical; he could answer the beggar who was asking for a *sou*: "My poor fellow, I have heard of such a coin, but never possessed one; here's a franc for you." Another day, he met on the pier an old London acquaintance, who had just come off the packet from England: "I am so glad to see you, for we heard in London that you were dead; the report was in general circulation when I left." "Mere stock-jobbing, my dear fellow, mere stock-jobbing!"

In July 1828 the Hon. George Dawson, c/o Mrs. Fitzherbert, Tilney Street, Port Lane, London, received the following letter:

Calais, July 20, 1828.

"My dear Dawson,

"Will you so far extend your usual kindness as to endeavour to be of instant service to me. It is not to yourself particularly that I take the liberty to address myself, for you must be very much changed, if you have any money at command; but to three or four of those former friends who you may think willing to stretch a point in my favour at the moment. I am in a serious scrape from my utter inability to provide for a rascally bill which had been long due, and which, if not paid on or before the 26th of this month, will expose me to the worst consequences—the amount is £73.

"Would you so essentially oblige me as to endeavour to gather together a few amiable Samaritans who might so kindly bear me and my actual difficulties in remembrance as to advance £25 each to satisfy this urgent demand? One hundred would relieve me and give me a few pounds over to scramble with. It would make me happy for the present.

"You are acquainted with the different things belonging to me, in China, Japan, etc. Select what you please to the amount of double the sum in question and it shall be faithfully sent to you or to anyone else in payment. I would sell myself if I could raise a shilling upon my worthless body and soul to be extricated from this predicament which really frightens me out of my wits.

"I wrote to Alvanley some time since acquainting him with my apprehensions about this bill, but I fear he is as usual without the means of assisting me. I have written to Worcester ten days since in the same sense as my present request to you, but I should think he is absent from Town, for I have received no answer from him, and time presses sorely upon me.

"I am, as you may have heard, expecting employment through the interference of the best of friends, the Duke of Wellington, but before such expectations may be realized I am sadly alarmed lest some overwhelming disaster should fall upon me.

Ever sincerely yours,
GEORGE BRUMMELL."

Another letter came in August.

Calais, Aug. 2nd, 1828.

"My dear Dawson,

"You are a very good fellow for answering my letter at all, but a most excellent one during a fit of the gout. What business have you to be tormented with gout? It would become me perhaps, for no one deserves it more for former "hard going" and here I am with uninterrupted good health and, I firmly believe, an unimpaired constitution. It is all, indeed, that is left to me, but I ought to be thankful.

"You, on the contrary, have always been rather of a temperate life and have no right to the Mala Podagra to disturb your days and nights. I would willingly sell or lend my limbs to anyone afflicted like yourself by way of exchange from other annoyances.

"Your kindness towards me gives me good spirits for the moment and I thank you with all my heart. For a long time past I have been unaccustomed to even friendly acknowledgements. Alvanley has sent me £50 through Drummonds. He does not like making further application to others, for speaking is always more effective than writing, or I might, perhaps, be relieved from the demands that press upon me. He is, however, the best judge of the grounds of such disinclination and I thank him equally as the steadiest friend I possess.

"There certainly is a vacancy in the Consular Department at Petersburgh, for though the present incumbent, Sir Something Bailey, is gone back there, I know he has tendered his resignation, and that Marshall, the Consul here, has several times written soliciting that preferment.

"Can you find out quietly whether it is the intention to place me here as Consul, or to send me elsewhere, of course a vacancy occurring to facilitate the business.

Ever yrs,

G.B."

The chance of obtaining a consular post became his only hope. From that moment he wrote to all his friends, urging them to endeavour to obtain for him this consulate at Calais. All visitors to Calais became the messengers of Brummell's plight. Charles Greville, who was Clerk of the Council and therefore in constant touch with the chiefs of all the parties, had a talk in December with Wellington and implored that "poor Brummell" be taken care of. The Duke explained to Greville that he had already attempted to do his utmost, but Lord Aberdeen had interposed, and the King was adamant on the subject of Brummell.

In the spring of 1829 Greville determined to visit the Beau. Poor Brummell was unaware that he was receiving a saviour angel, and kept Greville in his place, though expanding upon his hardships, but dwelling upon his indestructible hopes for the morrow. Greville entered these notes in his diary: "At Calais (March 6) I had a long conversation with Brummell about his consulship, and was moved by his account of his own distress to write to the Duke of Wellington and ask him to do what he could for him. I found him in his old lodging, dressing. Some pretty pieces of old furniture in the room, an entire toilet of silver, and a large green macaw perched on the back of a tattered silk chair with faded gilding; full of gaiety, impudence and misery. The parrot was called Hobhouse. "Doesn't he look exactly like Hobhouse?"

Only a few weeks previously that amusing and veracious traveller and profound judge of English society, Prince Pucker Muskan, who was wandering about Europe, found himself at Calais, and went to pay a visit to Brummell.

"Every bird of passage from the fashionable world dutifully pays the former patriarch the tribute of a visit, or of an invitation to dinner," he wrote. "This I did also, though under my assumed name. Unfortunately, in the matter of dinner I had been forestalled by another stranger; and I cannot therefore judge how a coat really ought to look; or whether his long residence in Calais, added to increasing years, have rendered the dress of the former King of Fashion less classical, for I found him at his second *toilette*, in a flowered chintz dressing-gown, velvet night-cap with gold tassel, and Turkish slippers, shaving, and rubbing the remains of his teeth with his favourite red root. The furniture of his rooms was elegant enough, part of it might even be called rich, though faded; and I cannot deny that the whole man seemed to me to correspond with it. Though depressed by his present situation, he exhibited a considerable fund of good humour and good nature. His air was that of good society, simple and natural, and marked by more urbanity than the Dandies of the present race are capable of. With a smile he showed me his Paris peruke, which he extolled at the cost of the English ones, and called himself, '*le ci-devant jeune homme qui passe sa vie entre Paris et Londres*'.

"He appeared somewhat curious about me, asked me questions concerning people and things in London, without belying his good breeding by any kind of intrusive-ness; and then took occasion to convince me that he was perfectly well informed as to all that was passing in the English world of fashion, as well as of politics. '*Je suis au courant de tout*,' he exclaimed, '*mais àquoi cela me sert-il? On me laisse mourir de faim ici. J'espère pourtant que mon ancien ami le Duc de Wellington enverra un beau jour le consul d'ici en Chine, et qu'ensuite il me nommera à sa place. Alors je suis sauvé.*' And surely the English nation ought in justice to do something for the man who invented starched cravats! How many did I see in London in the enjoyment of large sinecures, who had done far less for their country! As I took my leave, and was going down stairs, he opened the door, and called after me: '*J'espère que vous trouvez votre chemin; mon Suisse n'est pas là, je crains.*' '*Hélas,*' thought I, '*point d'argent, point de Suisse.*' "

Alas, a few months later neither the German prince nor Charles Greville would have found the fine pieces of old furniture. To meet the most urgent creditors, a sale of Buhl furniture was arranged, and it fetched a considerable sum. His Sèvres china had been bought some time before by the London auctioneer, Mr. Crockford, Jnr., who prompted by the Hon. George Dawson, went to Calais on purpose. Crockford described the porcelain as "the finest and purest ever imported into England". Indeed, at the sale George IV gave two hundred guineas for a tea-set, and a pair of vases was sold for three hundred pounds to the Duke of Buccleuch. But neither the Sèvres porcelain nor the Buhl furniture was sufficient to satisfy half his creditors' claims, for his banker's account alone stood at this time at twelve thousand francs on the debit side. Only in the consulate, Brummell's letters reminded his friends, could he now see his salvation!

VII

In such conditions there was only one comfort left for a man of spirits, and it was to fall in love. Brummell fell in love with a girl in her 'teens, whose irresistible attraction was that she had lovely eyebrows. She was a devout Roman Catholic, and for love of her, Brummell turned Catholic without delay. (It happened that the English residents of Calais were, at the moment, making a collection for building an Episcopal Chapel, and one of them knocked at Brummell's door: "I am sorry", the Beau answered, "that you did not call last week, for it was only yesterday that I became a Catholic—but never mind, put my name down for a hundred francs." And he had not a penny for himself!)

He wrote a letter in Werther's style to the young lady, who turned him down, offering him, the coquette, her friendship, if not love:

"Yesterday morning I was subdued almost to insanity; but your note in the evening restored me, and as if I had been redeemed from earthly purgatory, placed me in heaven. Thank you, thank you, dearest of beings; how can I requite all this benevolent open-heartedness, this delightful proof and avowal of my not being indifferent to you? By the dim light that was remaining I perceived something white at your *porte-cochère*. It was evident that I was recognized, and the figure advanced with your billet. In an instant I seized the hand of your faithful and intelligent messenger, compressing it forcibly. I should have saluted her, if I had not fancied at the instant that

I heard someone coming up the street. We parted, and I returned to my solitary chamber. There I lacerated the letter with impatience, and then the light of love and joy, and the refreshing breath of evening, stole through the open window over my entranced senses. After that I sought another stroll on the ramparts, and again returned home contented with you, with myself, and with the world. I have known few that could equal, none that could excel you; yet they possessed not your charms of countenance, your form, your heart, in my estimation. Certainly they did not possess that unaffected and fervent homage, which in my constant memory—in my heart's blood—and in my devoted soul I bear to you."

The rumour went round Calais that the young lady was "returning his passion", and the soulful British compatriots thought it fit to send a representative to ask Brummell for an explanation, "lest he should abduct her". They sent an elderly army officer from London. But the fellow had not gone far with his harangue, when Brummell looked him up and down: "Why, Vulcan, what a precious old humbug you must be, to come and lecture me on such a subject—you who were for two years at hide-and-seek to save yourself from being shot by Sir T.S. for running off with one of his daughters!"

On 26th June 1830 George IV died at Windsor looking, in the words of the Duchess of Gloucester, "like a feather bed". With the death of the King who had been the Regent, and the former friend and patron of Brummell, had disappeared the main obstacle to helping the ci-devant-Beau. Alvanley had never given up his determination to rescue his friend in Calais, and scarcely had the ceremonies for the accession of William IV died down, than he besieged the Duke of Wellington, still Prime

Minister, to reopen the subject. The appeal was duly made by Wellington; William IV barely remembered Brummell and at that not enthusiastically; but he was eager to oblige "the Duke", and on 10th September 1830, George Bryan Brummell was gazetted as British Consul at Caen. The salary was £400 a year.

When the news reached the exile in the Rue Royale at Calais, it was like being reborn. In broadcasting the news he said to all that "he owed his appointment entirely to the favourable consideration of the Commander-in-Chief". It did not matter if, all going well, the remainder of his days were to be devoted to the verification of passports, bills of lading, invoices and mercantile papers—indeed, Brummell did not inquire what his duties were likely to be!

His "elevation" to the consulate was, however, the source of fresh and urgent complications. For, if he was anxious to shake off the dust of Calais, his creditors were even more anxious to prevent his departure, at least not whilst there remained those strong bonds of indebtedness between him and them. There was the tailor, the upholsterers, the draper, the decorator, the jewellers, the bootmaker, the perruquier, even the valet and the washerwoman; and there was the banker!

The two tailors Pion and Lamotte were merely tyros in the art and were only entrusted with repairs, the principal artist being Gaussin, who had been a prisoner in England during the wars, and Brummell had taught him the essentials in the art of cutting a coat. The chemist's bills were mostly for *huile antique* and cold cream; and the consumption of 176 francs of oils and cold cream was a pretty example of the extravagance of Brummell's habit in his *toilette*—but there it was. And all the bills had to be paid, or at least settled to the suppliers' and creditors' satisfaction.

Brummell found a wonderful saviour in the banker, Monsieur Leveux. Even upon a hardened French banker the charm of George Brummell had worked wonders. Besides, in the course of years, M. Leveux had seen considerable sums pass through his bank for Brummell, always sums, as one could say, descending from heaven, such as might be the case for a king in exile. And Brummell had frequently sent his visiting friends to M. Leveux to cash their bills. The banker agreed, therefore, to liquidate Brummell's creditors at Calais and enable him to proceed to Caen and take up his official duties. A list of the liabilities was drawn, as follows:

	Francs
To his valet, François Sélègne, for house expenses and etceteras ..	6,162
Bill at Dessein's for dinners	3,488
Lefêvre, hatter	54
Lamotte and Pion, tailors	373
Baudron and Samson, chemists ..	176
Lafond Bressell, Bonvarlet, Lemoine, upholsterers	75
Parque Waillier, draper	309
Ducastel, decorator of ceilings ..	24
Desjardins and Boissard, jewellers ..	35
Fasquel, bootmaker	150
Piedfort, perruquier	8
Washerwoman	100
Fille de chambre	50
Isaac Pecquet, banker	500
	11,504

M. Leveux was willing to advance twelve thousand francs and to remove all impediments to the departure.

Brummell, on the other hand, to guarantee M. Leveux repayment of this sum which was in addition to the twelve thousand already overdrawn, made over to M. Leveux, by letter of assignment to Mr. Hertslett, of the Foreign Office, three hundred and twenty pounds per annum, being all but eighty of his salary as Consul. It was very hazardous to set upon an official career with but the prospects of £80 a year; but Brummell did not feel any fear for the future; and towards the end of September 1830, he left the city of Calais where he had vegetated for fourteen years. He was in the best of spirits. Through the friendship of his friend the Consul at Calais, Mr. Marshall, he was travelling to Paris with a King's messenger, and of course free of expense. The silver-greyhound was a very aristocratic Mercury, who duly appreciated the honour of travelling with so celebrated a person as Beau Brummell.

The only memory Brummell was regretful of leaving behind was the screen which he had worked with his own hands for the lamented Duchess of York; the screen was subsequently pawned by the valet, François Sélègne with an upholsterer at Boulogne, who still had it when Captain Jesse visited the town in search of Brummell's memoirs.

VIII

It was grand to be in Paris, en route for his Consulship at Caen. Perhaps it was better still not to have been to Paris before—just to have lived there in the aura of his former glory.

They received him like a man who had been a king—"King by grace of Grace". He stayed at the British Embassy, guest of his old friend of better days, Lord Stuart de Rothesay, who was Ambassador. He graced the streets of Paris for a whole week, and was entertained by the *haute volée* of the capital. Louis Philippe had appointed Talleyrand Ambassador to England, but the Prince of Benevento had not yet left Paris, and the old rogue, who had found it easy to serve both Napoleon and Louis XVIII, entertained Brummell as a "confrère". At seventy-four Talleyrand, with a solitary strand of white hair sweeping down on one side, was more than ever self-assured, cynical and humorous, and at the palace of Talleyrand the cuisine was perfect, for he was wont to say that he was kept alive by his cook rather than by his doctor.

To meet Talleyrand was to meet everyone that mattered in Paris. Thus Brummell met the Comte Louis Molé, who was Foreign Secretary, and gave him letters for the Prefect of Caen; and he met Comte Casimir de Montrond, who was Talleyrand's shadow, his petted pupil and confidant, gay, frivolous, gambling, of no morals whatever. On being asked by a Princess of the Imperial family why he was so attached to his great protector Talleyrand, he replied with an air of *naïveté*: "How can one help loving him? He is so deliciously full of vice!"

Montrond had no political ambition, honours and places did not tempt him; but he was fond of money, not to hoard it, only to lavish it. He made money by wisely investing the State secrets that his friends whispered to him. On one occasion, by a little secret operation he realized a clear two million francs. "Now you are rich," Talleyrand told him, "where shall you put this two millions?" "Why, where should I?" said Montrond. "In my *secrétaire*, of course." Nor did the two millions rest there a long time.

Yes, Brummell found Montrond an amusing fellow; and he was delighted to be fêted by the Princess de Bagration. It was indeed like the old times, when he was a favourite of the Duchess of Devonshire.

He also contrived to examine all the snuff-boxes in the Palais Royal and the Rue de la Paix, but not one was worthy of his selection, and before leaving Paris, he ordered one at Dabert's; a gold box, exquisitely enamelled, for the trifling sum of two thousand five hundred francs —it was more than one year's salary, but what mattered?

On the 5th of October Brummell arrived in Caen, in a post-chaise hired in Paris for the occasion, with his valet, François Sélègne in the rumble, four horses and two pos-tillions: amid the *feu d'artifice* of their whips he entered the *porte cochère* of the Hotel de la Victoire, and to the cook (whom he mistook for the landlord) he ordered "the best room, the best dinner, and the best Laffitte". Then he signed the register "His Britannic Majesty's Consul". He felt, indeed, that now life was beginning afresh.

A week later, however, he removed to private lodgings:

the Hotel de la Victoire (that still stands near the market-place) was no place fit for the Britannic Consul: and as Brummell wrote in a letter to Marshall, the Consul in Calais: "Stuart and several of my friends in Paris have spoilt me for at least one year to come." The Hotel de la Victoire was "one of the worst hotels, I am confident, in Europe", not could he endure to "gnaw bones upon un-washed dowlas".

Good fortune led his steps to "an admirable lodging, half a house, the property of a most cleanly, devout old lady, excellently furnished, with a delightful garden, two Angora cats and a parrot that I have already thrown into apoplectic fits with sugar".

The house was in the Rue des Carmes; it was a digni-fied building with a neat frontage of grey stone, three stories high with the typical French mansardes for a fourth above the roof, and the first floor above the *rez-de-chaussée*, which was the *piano nobile*, adorned with small balconies of wrought iron at each window, properly screened by lace curtains. A most gentlemanly residence.

Moreover, the house belonged to Madame de Guernon de Saint Ursain, *née* Aimable Ange Vastin. As a child, Mademoiselle Vastin, who was of Dutch birth, had been adopted by two old maids called de Guernon Ranville and had married their cousin M. de Guernon, a relative of that Monsieur Ranville who was Minister of Charles X and was incarcerated for several years in the Castle of Ham with Polignac and his fellow-conspirators.

In the *salon* of Madame de Saint Ursain were to be found the best society of Caen: M. de Saint Quentin, M. de Vanquelin, M. de Sainte Marie, M. de Roncherolles, all sipping tea *à l'anglaise* and reviling the Jacobin tendencies of *le roi-citoyen* Philippe-Egalité, and whispering their great hopes of the Duc de Bordeaux. All this was very attractive for Brummell, so reminiscent of London; and Madame de Saint Ursain was soon enchanted with His Majesty's Consul. Furthermore she told Brummell immediately that he could pay his rent when he would, and this was an item that Consul Brummell appreciated to the full.

His valet François, having initiated his successor in his duties, made his bow and departed. This man Sélègne certainly did not lose by attending to Brummell for fourteen years; for he appeared for an extraordinary large sum in the list of creditors that Brummell left in Calais; and after his return to that town he removed to Boulogne, and with the money he had saved in Brummell's service, set up a "Café Sélègne" in the Grand Rue, and later he opened a hotel, till the invasion of Napoleon III exploded his hopes and Sélègne had to revert to the more simple business of *cafétier*.

Brummell had barely taken possession of his new lodging in the Rue des Carmes than he found his table "inundated" with invitations and visiting cards: the Prefect, Monsieur Target (who was the son of the avocat that refused the benefit of his legal assistance to Louis XVI when called to defend that unfortunate king), the General and three or four other big-wigs for whom Brummell had been given letters by Comte Molé and Comte Sebastiani. He found himself a great man, even if he did not have a sixpence in his pocket. They dined and fêted him most liberally, and elected him a member of their club without a ballot. The Prefect and the local Member of Parliament, Monsieur de la Pommeraye, gave a great dinner in honour of the new Britannic Consul, and Brummell prepared "a neat little extempore" in which he let off a toast to the success of the commerce between the two countries.

He invented a kind of costume as Consul: for the morning he chose a snuff-coloured coat with a velvet collar a shade darker, and a waistcoat of washable cashmere on a white ground, cut from a lady's shawl; and encased within this original waistcoat emerged the foamy whiteness of his dazzling cravat. With this brown and white rigout he wore dark blue trousers and pointed boots, primrose kid gloves and a very high black topper the crown of which was slightly larger than the base: the style of the topper has become for ever the hallmark of the elegant man.

In the evening he changed to Whig colours of his London days; blue coat with velvet collar, buff waistcoat and black trousers. On the lapel of his coat he fixed the consular button.

Truly, his capacity to stand out among and above other men, almost to rule, seemed to survive every vicissitude. His exile and his financial disarrangements in London and in Calais had passed over his head without disturbing one single hair. Empires had risen and fallen while he experimented with the folds of his necktie and the cut of his coats. And his health, like his taste, was never at fault.

If his appointment to the Consulate was considered most flattering to the city of Caen, his entry into the town had been truly sensational. With his usual flair, Brummell exploited the situation to the full. Invested, nay, protected by his official position, he found a new amusement in giving vent to his impertinence. A few days after he had taken up residence in the Rue des Carmes, three worthy gentlemen of Caen paid him a morning visit, and found him, though late in the day, busy with all the mysteries of his *toilette*. The three gentlemen were anxious to retire immediately, but Brummell airily waved a hand: "Pray stay, Messieurs, pray remain; I have not yet breakfasted—no excuses; there is a *pâté de foie gras*, a *pain de gibier*, and many other dainties." But the three *bon vivants* of Caen modestly felt that they must not take advantage of such politeness and hospitality; and however attractive the conversation, they departed. Of course, there was no *pain de gibier* on the breakfast sideboard nor *pâté de foie gras*; Brummell had invented them counting on the extreme improbability of their accepting his invitation!

His brilliancy, the point of impertinence in his conversation was indeed irresistible; and he pressed it impartially against both the French and English society of Caen. The English, indeed—and there was quite a large number of English in the town—continually pestered him with their civilities merely to satisfy their vanity, by being able to "show" him in their drawing-rooms. Brummell, who saw through it, aired his sarcastic remarks, even among the fair sex.

There was a lady, daughter-in-law of the local English doctor; rather a pretty woman, but always aping the great lady. One day, as Brummell and a friend were passing under the balcony at which the lady, like an ordinary *bourgeoise*, was fanning herself, her mellifluous voice came down: "Good evening, Mr. Brummell." The gentlemen stopped, raised their heads, and Brummell's companion also raised his hat; not so Brummell, who had already sufficiently discomposed the folds of his cravat by looking up; and they were on the point of resuming their walk, when the voice came down again: "Now won't you come up and take tea?" For a moment Brummell stood speechless; then he raised again his grey eyes, so *petillant d'ésprit*, so full of laughter, and addressed the following pithy and impudent remark to the lady on the first-floor front:

"Madam, you take medicine, you take a walk, you take a liberty, but you *drink* tea." This he was determined not to do, certainly not with the little lady on the first-floor front; and proceeded on his way.

He was, in fact, in that first year of Consulship in Caen, a walking lampoon, and his sarcastic vein was very droll and amusing to those who were not, at the moment, the victims of his satire; but they all knew that each in turn would be served up for the amusement of his neighbours.

A French family gave a dinner, almost in his honour, and everything had been done to make it perfect—the ortolans from Toulouse, the salmon from Rouen, and the company were Legitimists. The morning after someone asked Brummell how the dinner had passed off. He lifted up his hands, shook his head: "Don't ask me, my good fellow; but poor man, he did his best."

IX

It lasted six months—but what a time it was! Caen was not London, but it was a little world in itself, and for Brummell it was his Hundred Days.

During those six months, indeed, towards the end, in February 1832, Captain Jesse, back to worldly life after six years in India, enamoured of the Beau whose fame had spread as far as the eastern outposts, paid a visit to Caen, anxious to meet George Bryan Brummell in person.

The first encounter—and the result of that meeting was all important, for the young Captain was to turn out a Boswell to Brummell—the first encounter took place in a Mrs. B——'s drawing-room.

Jesse had never seen Brummell before; yet, although he entered the drawing-room with several other visitors, the extreme neatness of his person, the polished ease of his address, something peculiarly striking at once pointed him out. It was quite pleasing to see the graceful manner in which he made his way through the crowded *salon* up to the hostess, the deep bow with which he saluted her, almost a particular tribute to her. His bow to each of the other ladies was graduated according to the degree of intimacy that existed between them; the bow to his friends being at an angle of forty-five degrees, while a common acquaintance was acknowledged by one of five; some were greeted with a slight relaxation of his features expressing his recognition of the fact that she was an inhabitant of the same planet as himself.

He had all the *bel air*, all the *tournure* of a man of

fashion. His dress, on the evening in question, consisted of a blue coat with a velvet collar, and the consular button and buff waistcoat, black trousers and boots. His tie was unsurpassable, and his *blanchisseuse* had certainly done her best in the getting up: besides, Brummell always gave careful instruction to his washerwoman how she was to fold the cloth of his cravats, and one single speck would send them back to the soapsuds.

The only articles of jewellery he wore were a plain ring and a massive chain of Venetian ducat gold, which served as a guard to his watch: only two links were to be seen, those that passed from the buttons of his waistcoat to the pocket. It was a peculiar chain of the same pattern as those suspended outside the entrance to Newgate prison. The ring, however, was dug up on the Field of Cloth of Gold by a labourer, who sold it to Brummell when he was at Calais. An opera hat and gloves that were held in his hand, completed an attire which could never have attracted attention on any other person. But that was the point—his appearance was noticeable only for its extreme neatness and for the way he carried his clothes. One evening, when Captain Jesse had become more intimate, they found themselves at the same dining-table, and Brummell gently admonished his friend: "My dear Jesse, I am sadly afraid you must have been reading *Pelham*; but excuse me, you look very much like a magpie!" Jesse did indeed, for he was dressed in a black coat and trousers with a white waistcoat.

Jesse has recorded minutely the ritual of Brummell at his *toilette* that he was privileged to witness many times. The *batterie de toilette* was of silver, and elaborate in its details: there still was a silver spitting-dish of the same size as a French wash-hand basin, therefore not very large: and Brummell had pointed out to his friend that "it was impossible to spit in clay". After his shaving was over—a shaving performed with the smallest possible razor—two hours were spent in ablutions.

The door of his bedroom was always left a little open to carry on conversation, and the secrets of his dressing-table were revealed in the glass upon the mantelpiece of his *salon*. He used to stand before the glass, not wearing his wig, in his dressing trousers, massaging his body with a stiff brush of bristle something like the strigil used by Petronius, to regenerate his epidermis; when he had done with it, as red as a lobster, he was ready for the camisole. But before dressing—or rather robing himself—Brummell took a dentist's mirror in one hand and a pair of tweezers in the other, and closely examined his forehead and well-shaved chin, and he did not lay the tweezers down till he had mercilessly plucked every stray hair that could be detected on the polished surface of his face. (Jesse never let Brummell know that he had seen him in the reflection of the mirror, without his wig.) At last, completely dressed, every hair in its right place, his cravat a perfection of folds, his exquisite white cashmere waistcoat beautifully contrasting with his snuff-coloured day-coat, which he always kept buttoned up to accentuate the waist, with his primrose gloves on his hands, and an umbrella under his arm, his body slightly bent and his tie reflected in his lucent boots, he emerged from the house and proceeded, at a very slow pace, either to make a morning call or to kill the interval till dinner by lounging with an acquaintance in the Rue St. Jean.

He had now discarded the cane, perhaps because Caen was often visited by rain, and he was carrying regularly a brown silk umbrella, which was always protected by a silk case that fitted as accurately as his own coat. The handle was surmounted by a head of George IV carved in ivory. In the street he never took off his hat to anyone, not even to a lady; it would have been too difficult to replace it at the prescribed angle, added to which, his wig might be disturbed. In fine weather the salute of his associates was acknowledged by a bow or, if the acquaintances were on the other side of the street, by an extension of his arm, and a slight movement of his fingers in the air.

The most entertaining thing, however, was to see him walking in rainy or muddy weather. As there were no side-paths, he was too much occupied with his lower extremities to think of noticing anything but the uneven paving stones: he always placed his foot on the highest ones, and so cleverly did he pick his way on the points of his toes that he contrived to travel the whole length of the street without contracting one speck of dirt on his boots, the soles of which were always polished. When his new friend Jesse walked with him on a rainy day, he always desired him to "keep his distance", lest the friend's more careless tread should splash his trousers and his boots.

During those six months Brummell enjoyed life, and society, to the full. He was the Consul, he was an official personage, there was almost a touch of childish pleasure in thinking of himself as "official", after the dreary years of want and worry at Calais! And he could run up a bill; the creditors, for the moment, felt honoured.

The ladies of Caen were almost as good as the ladies of London: there was a conservative refinement in those provincial drawing-rooms. And occasionally there came to Caen ladies from London: who was the English lady to whom he had sworn "by those humble ancestors who sleep in their parish churchyards" that he would never reveal her as the authoress of the lines on the "toilet-table drawer"? He had added the verses to his album; and as she was demanding of him something in return,

Brummell sent her his sketch of the late Georgiana of Devonshire, with a note containing a hint that they should meet the same day: "I am ashamed to send you so unworthy a sketch of a beautiful woman. Do not unjustly fancy that you are for a moment forgotten, because I do not immediately remit to you my relics of past times in writing or in crayon. You shall have others as I go on, unwillingly digging in old green boxes. The sun shines bright, and promises me the consolation of meeting you in your morning's whereabouts. Yours forever and ever, Amen!"

He dallied with the Caen ladies, he wrote them charming letters, with delightful endings: "Ineffably yours", "Most sensibly yours". Once a letter must have reached the recipient in a greasy state, on hearing of which this note was sent in all haste: "Do, in compassion to my inveterate *propreté*, send back the sullied envelope that contained my last packet, and accept this explanatory *billet*. The gloves which delivered it were spick and span; but alas it must have visited your kitchen, and that explains the blemish; yet, I give you my word, I took no liberties *avec la cuisinière. . . .*"

There was Madame du Lac, a perfect Lady of the Lake, with the sweetest face and the daintiest foot in that part of France. There was the *Générale*, who gave *soirées musicales*, the dullness of which was relieved by the General's and other amateur singing; and Madam de Rigny who was the wife of the Minister of Marine's brother, who in Caen received the taxes while his wife received the company.... So delightfully provincial *et sur quatre épingles*! Brummell's own recording of it all in his letters is a gem:

"Madame de —— will be *charmée* to receive the 'black Infanta'; shall I send a palanquin for her, or will you pass her *en panier*? Madame de Lac tells me that the artiste for whom you inquired perfectly understands his *métier*, and that his *ressemblances sont frappantes*. I have already forgotten his name—as one does everything when talking to her, but he sojourns at the Hotel de France.

"D'Ison's convocation very good last night: all the brilliants of Babylon dazzling in their best: Mademoiselle ——, the prototype of Madame de la Vallière, when she took the veil.... Never doubt, as Hamlet says, I am thine."

Madame de St. Ursain had a young daughter, Hélène, now a pupil in the Caen's English school of a Miss Wheatcroft. Brummell undertook to teach the young lady of Rue des Carmes how to write his language. His method was to write to "Miss Aimable" long letters and to correct her replies and to go over the exercises which she brought home from school. "Miss Aimable" was only fourteen years of age, and Brummell's letters to her were a model of gentleness: "You have promised to take a lesson with me tomorrow morning, Christmas Day! What a period of rejoicing and fête, according to the customs of my native country, this used to be to me, some years since, while now of joys that are past, how painful the remembrance!" And again: "Dear Miss Aimable, the study of English is no doubt valuable, but the duties of kindness must not be neglected for it. For more than a week I have seen no fresh straw in Ourika's basket, while Tigre is allowed to torment the parrot to death. I would rather preserve my feelings of humanity and tenderness for these mute creatures than acquire all the languages in the world."

The evenings in society, the gossiping letters, the exquisite clothes and the three changes of shirts and cravats a day, all were his escape from reality—and reality was already knocking hard on his door. The exquisite clothes and three changes a day of shirts, cravats and all the other frumperies of elegance and elegant living, all this cost a lot more than Brummell's meagre income afforded. It had been easy to get out of Calais clean of debts; but he had also got out of Calais, as thoughtless as a bird, right clean of his official salary. By mortgaging to the banker Leveux four-fifths of his 10,000 francs of yearly salary, he had reduced his income to a mere 200 francs a month, a pittance for Brummell. It was very nice to be able to tell young Captain Jesse that he always went home to put on a fresh cravat after the Opera before attending a ball or supper; but the *blanchisseuse*'s bill grew up accordingly, and the washerwoman's bill was only one in the many items that meant money, money, money.

Money troubles had started, indeed, almost immediately after his arrival at Calais. With fertile resourcefulness Brummell thought at once of Leveux, and tried to restart business connections with his friend and creditor of Calais. "*Mon cher Monsieur*," he wrote in April 1831, "*je ne croyez guères il y a six mois me trouver encore exposé à l'extremité de recourir à votre bonté.*" He had counted too much on the promises of his friends, and maybe it would be another long century of five or six months before his friends would please themselves to pull him out of his present position. Would, in the meantime, Monsieur Leveux consider it expeditious to help him out? "It is not for luxuries I am concerned; it is not for the pleasures of life, which I had to give up long ago; but it is a question, at the moment, of my honour, my reputation, and all my interests present and future, since I begin to fear a total lack of means of providing even the official expenses that fall daily upon me for the running of the Consulate."

In all truth, his friends in London had made no promises at all; indeed, having seen him, through all their efforts, properly settled in the Consulate with a handsome salary, and never imagining the fantastic arrangement of Calais, they rather congratulated themselves on their deliverance. The banker Leveux did not reply very speedily, and Brummell wrote again: "I have been in hopes for a month to receive your good news. Pushed to the extreme and to avoid my being chased about by the people of the town, to save in a word, the coat from my back, which is, in pure truth, all that is left me. . . ."

This second letter had the desired effect; Leveux cashed a bill equal to the first four months of the salary, "to meet the difficult century", pending help from the friends in London. But Caen was not Calais, on the high road between London and Paris, and passing friends could not be acquainted of his plight.

It was at this point that there entered upon the scene Mr. Armstrong. Charles Armstrong, of the fashionable Rue St. Jean, was a general man of business in Caen: he served the local English colony as grocer, tea merchant, packet agent, house agent and dealer in foreign exchange. Brummell had met him at the house of several acquaintances; and Armstrong was quite glad, almost flattered to be of some assistance to Consul Brummell, who had, most readily, been of some assistance to him in his official capacity. So in August we have the first letter from Brummell to Armstrong.

August 1831.

"Dear Armstrong,

"I have been reduced to so low an ebb during the last three weeks, by delay, and not receiving promised remittances from England, that it is impossible for me to hold up my head, or to exist in my actual state a day longer. For ten days I have actually not had five francs in my possession, and I have not the means of procuring either wood or peat for my scanty fire, or of getting my things from the washerwoman. A trifling advance would arrange these difficulties, and give me further time, but I know not who to apply to in this place.

"You have as yet been a good friend to me, and may have sufficient confidence in me, and inclination to extend some additional timely service to me. What I have already assured you I now repeat, with every honourable intention and feeling, you will not repent your kindness.

"I have not anything to offer you by way of security, excepting my signature, if it is not my small stock of plate, for which I paid six hundred francs, and my watch and chain, worth as much more; to these you are welcome, only do not let me be exposed to the most utter distress and want, from my temporary inability to command a few miserable francs. I am not going out, and if you can spare five minutes in the course of the morning, you will oblige me by coming down here: these matters are better arranged in person than by writing.

Yours,
G.B."

Armstrong settled with the most pressing creditors and declined to take away the offered security. But a short time afterwards another and more urgent letter was sent to Armstrong. The valet, Isidore, successor to the more loyal François, had soon found out that his exquisite master had no money at all, and became impertinent; gave notice and threatened to open the trenches of the law.

"Dear Armstrong,

"That d——d ungrateful brute, Isidore, persecutes me at every instant: the fellow says he is going to Paris on Thursday, and will not depart without being paid, in money or by bill, and I believe him capable of employing a *huissier*.

"I am wretchedly bedevilled, and out of spirits, and hate

going out of the house, or I would call and thank you for
your note of yesterday.

Truly yours,

G.B."

Once more Armstrong obliged; this time, however, he
accepted a gold watch with chain and seals for his favour.

Two Caen bankers, Messrs. Gilbert & Bellamy, followed in the pertinacious Isidore's wake; with Armstrong's
signature they agreed to stave off for a season.

Ready money, nevertheless, was absolutely necessary
at times, to stop the proceedings of some importune creditor, or to provide to the daily disbursements of Brummell's menage; once again Armstrong of the Rue St. Jean
has to come to the rescue:

"Dear Armstrong,

"I am positively pressed for two hundred and eighty
francs, at the moment, that is, before four o'clock today,
or I shall be exposed to the utmost disgrace. The things,
that is, the plate, are in the closet in my room, and you
may have them by sending any confidential person for
them; but I do not like to trust my servant with them, as
it may be known, or she may be seen with them in the
street. It is the urgency of the moment that I am anxious to
weather; small difficulties often extend to irreparable destruction of character; such is my situation at this instant.

Yours,

G.B."

But this time Mr. Armstrong walked out of the house
in the Rue des Carmes with the box of silver cutlery.

Only his landlady, Madame de St. Ursain, played the
Good Samaritan: she was lenient with Brummell, and as

her lodger forgot to pay, she pretended to forget that he owed the rent—like the bookseller Leleux at Calais, who would have kept him for nothing if only he had stayed, happy to find the value of his rent in the amusing conversation of his tenant, so Madame de St. Ursain felt that Mr. Brummell was such a distinguished gentleman; it was an honour to have him in her house!

But would the ladies of Caen ever have espied from Brummell's countenance his worries and troubles? He chatted with them, he discussed with them in his letters and *billets* the latest books: "Have you read the *American Journey* of Fanny Kemble? I begin to grow a little weary of her artificial sentiment, and particularly of all the I's which overload her recollections." And he criticizes Lady Blessington, the patroness of the new star of fashion, the handsome and fortunate Comte d'Orsay: "Her novel, *The Two Friends*, will bore you to death. Lady Blessington, now that her beauty is vanishing, has become over-saintly, like all aristocratic penitents. . . ."

One April morning, however, Brummell is startled by his faithful Madame de St. Ursain, who in great agitation comes up to his rooms to tell him that downstairs, at the door of the house, are two bailiffs who are threatening to break into his rooms. Hurriedly the good lady urges Brummell to hide, opens a cupboard in her adjoining room and pushes him in amidst a confusion of gowns and crinolines. . . . Brummell shudders at such undignified expediency but does not lose his presence of mind, and from flounces and lace calls out to the dear helpmate: "Madame de St. Ursain! For mercy's sake, take away the key!"

The position is now getting quite precarious. Brummell finds that his position as Consul at Caen is not, after all, much of a situation. The salary is small, the town is

petty, the duties are trivial. He has heard that his col-
league at Le Havre, Mr. Gordon, is retiring: why not
apply for the post? Or better still, why not try to be sent
to Italy, at Leghorn, where the living is cheap and the
climate delightful?

Lord Palmerston—whom he used to meet, in the great
old days, at Harriette Wilson's (confound the harlot!)—
is now at the Foreign Office, and is all powerful. He has
no particular claim on him, it is true, for Palmerston was
a Harrovian, not an Etonian like himself; but still. . . .

Brummell wrote to Lord Palmerston: to clothe his
petition in dignity he explained, almost complained of the
paucity and triviality of his work in the Caen Consulate.

It was a great blunder. For it was a bad moment to
complain to Palmerston of the paucity of work in any
consulate: the Government were about to send an expedi-
tionary force into Afghanistan, and the Foreign Secretary
was looking around to find the funds. Instead of taking up
Brummell's hint of transfer to a busier post, Palmerston
replied with a chilly letter, inquiring purely whether
there was any necessity for a consulate at Caen. Brummell made a second and fatal mistake. He replied:

"Your lordship must be aware that by informing the
Government of the inutility of a consul at Caen, I am
actuated by purely disinterested motives. Your lordship
will also bear in mind that my bread depends upon the
trifling emolument which I receive as consul at Caen.
Should your lordship, therefore, on my suggestion, think
fit to abolish the office, I trust some means of subsistence
will be provided for me by the Government."

Lord Palmerston thanked Brummell for the information, made great promises, but for the moment abolished
the Consulate at Caen. Brummell was left on the rocks.
Disaster was imminent.

PART FOUR

The Last Reception

I

He should have died young. His life should have ended with an accident, a dramatic episode. He would then have died in the full glory of his legend. Instead, from this moment he became merely a poor man.

From the time that it was reported that he was no longer the representative of His British Majesty in Caen, his creditors rushed to the door in the Rue des Carmes. The first and the fiercest, was a Monsieur Longuet, who kept a restaurant from which at times Brummell had his meals sent in. Monsieur Longuet claimed a credit of 1,200 francs; and he swore that he would have him arrested if he left the house, or would starve him if he kept to the house. The siege was raised by a group of young men, who were good customers of Monsieur Longuet, and going immediately to the shop they informed him that if he attempted to molest the unfortunate debtor, they would never dine again at his place.

At this stage Brummell made the error of professing himself an out-and-out Carlist; and this lost him the sympathies of the officialdom and of those useful people whom he had called "the tradesmen of the Prefecture".

Quite soon he found himself without a *sous* in his purse. "Dear Armstrong," said the note he sent in great hurry, "send me seventy-five francs to pay my washerwoman; I cannot get a shirt from her, and she is really starving on my account. I have not actually money to pay my physician, or for my letters to and from England."

Armstrong complied once more. But how could the

position be faced? There was still the equivalent of one
year's salary owing to Leveux in Calais, and no salary
was coming in. And Brummell felt a sorrowful regret for
the good Madame de St. Ursain to whom he had never
paid anything in rent but for a paltry 600 francs. The
least he could do was to leave the pleasant rooms in the
Rue de Carmes and move to some cheaper lodgings.

He should never have left the house of Madame de St.
Ursain; he should not have detached himself from the
friendly house in this hour of need. Yet, he felt that however callous he could be with his phalanx of surly creditors, he owed this act of gentlemanly decency to the good
and charming Madame de St. Ursain.

He found rooms *au troisième* at the Hotel d'Angleterre,
where he would be *en pension*, dining at the table d'hôte;
and in September 1832 he came away from the Rue des
Carmes. He was so heartbroken that although he had to
pass Madame de St. Ursain's drawing-room, he could not
face going in to say good-bye. Some months later in the
new year, he knocked at her door and when the good lady
reminded him that he had gone away without bidding her
adieu, he took her hand and confessed to her: "Madame
de St. Ursain, I would have willingly wished you good-
bye, but I was in tears."

Soon after his change of lodgings, in the autumn, his
distress became so acute that he accepted the advice contained in a friend's letter, that it would be much wiser to
have his embarrassments explained in person to his
friends by a man of business, and he induced Armstrong
to go to London on his behalf. The friend—"a good angel
in London"—added: "I don't know how to get at the
Duke of Wellington or Lord Willoughby, but I will write
to George Anson and his brother Litchfield, to Bagot, Al-

vanley and many others that may occur to me, and among them, by the way, old Allen who, I assure you, spoke of you the other day in the kindest manner. . . ."

Armstrong took boat for England in mid-autumn. But as soon as his friend and man-of-business had gone, Brummell's spirits flagged. Would his friends of St. James's turn a cold shoulder to the returning tale of his misfortunes? Thus brooding in his lonely rooms, he was taken ill, and one Sunday evening while he was writing a letter to the sweet "Miss Aimable" to keep her in practice with her English, but much more, to pour out the loneliness of his heart—"Oh, this uncomfortable weather! I am freezing *au coin de mon feu*, and you must not, then, in common compassion, expect either amusement or instruction from a *malheureux* in my torpid state. There are moments, too, when I am subject to that sort of overwhelming depression of spirits that makes me incapable of anything but to brood over my own grievances—*le plus grand des malheurs est celui de ne tenir à rien, et d'être isolé*. I am sick of the world and of existence. . . ." At this point the pen dropped from his hand, he felt a giddiness, and then his right side went numb, and as he tried to get up and call for help, his voice, to a servant that chanced to pass the door, sounded thick and unnatural. It was a stroke. A doctor was quickly summoned, who bled and comforted him, and made no mention of the paralysis he knew it to be.

It was a joy to hear that so many friends were inquiring after him; and as soon as he could hold the pen again, he wrote witty notes to the ladies. But to Madame de St. Ursain he opened his heart more fully: "I have risen to-day with my head perfectly quiet, my chest and all its vicinity composed and free from those excruciating spasms which I thought, and at one time sacrilegiously prayed, would put an end to my sufferings in this world. . . ."

A few days later he was well enough to go to a wedding. And, soon afterwards, Armstrong returned from England, the harbinger of welcome, oh, how welcome news! Armstrong had been a persuasive suppliant, and all the old friends had rallied to the help of "poor Brummell reduced to two small rooms on the third floor of a cheap hotel in Caen". The Duke of Wellington, George Anson and his brother, Alvanley, Bagot, Allen, Coventry and Worcester, and others too, made donations to the fund, Burlington, Pembroke, Standish and Charles Greville the diarist. Each had placed, so to speak, his willing donation into Mr. Armstrong's hat, in memory of having enjoyed the favour of Brummell's friendship, in the years gone by.

Armstrong proceeded at once to put things in order according to the long list prepared before his departure, and commencing with the rent due to the good Madame de St. Ursain. With the banker Leveux he reached a temporary compromise, and the most pressing creditors were paid off. In the new year Brummell is again the Beau in full swing and attends the balls. To the ladies he recommends Beckford's *Letters from Paris*, and to Madame de St. Ursain he sends as a new year's gift a modest present: a knife for cutting bread and butter at her morning breakfast, with a mother-of-pearl handle: "I wish it consisted of one genuine pearl! Korizaida is a beautiful modern Greek name which Byron mentioned as often among the 'native seraphs' of those soft classic isles—its construction is Cluster of Pearls; should you be disposed to change your own, it would, in metaphor, be appropriate to you all.

"For many days I have not transgressed the wicket of my cell before vespers—I sit *en Calmouk*, enveloped in sable, musing over the fire like a poet in distress and ruminate upon other times and fairy prospects that will never come again. I was up to a dissipated hour this

morning, playing at five-*sous* whist with Madame d'A——.
Improvident pursuit! She made half-closed eyes at me,
instead of attending to the game; this afflicted me afterwards with a *cauchemar*: I fancied, in a dream, I was
struggling with my Aunt Margaret's ghost. I am still dor-
mant, and only just able to whisper to you how sincerely
I am yours. . . ."

The lady of the sentimental glances was a diminutive
wizen of a countess, who took quantities of snuff, and
wrote satirical verses on the manners of the *juste milieu*
and sonnets to the youthful Henri Cinq. And she was
wont to say: "*Ah, Monsieur, que nos salons sont tristes! Je ne
m'y connais plus. Dans ma jeunesse, une femme avait ses amis,
et son mari les siennes; chacun s'amusait selon sa manière: à
present on voit les époux toujours ensembles! Ah! qu'il sont
vilains les usages d'aujordhui.*"

Is it very silly for a man of fifty to fall in love with a
girl of seventeen? He had known Madame de St. Ursain's
daughter when she was a child of fifteen; now she was a
young woman of seventeen, and, in those times, many a
girl of fifteen was even being married to a man old enough
to be her grandfather. He had treated her as a little pupil
to whom he was imparting lessons in his beautiful and
witty English, and had received in return her admiration. Now there was little left to be admired, in a poor
sick and disenchanted Beau—the wreck of George Brummell; and he discovered that he was in love with a prim
and winsome young girl. How silly, and how foolish; and
yet, how sweet to write a tender love letter to "Miss
Aimable" who has gone to the sea at Luc-sur-Mer!

Tuesday, July.
"Millions of thanks to you for *Ayesha*. I have not quite

finished with her; for I cannot now read, nor write, nor do anything in a methodical way; therefore I return her to you, with every expression of admiration for your mutual excellences; with *Ayesha*, indeed, I have only made a transitory acquaintance—you I know already by heart.

"Why, in the name of common prudence and my own tranquillity, could I not have been contented to restrict my knowledge of you to the worldly etiquette of taking off my hat to you, when we casually met? During those years that I have vegetated upon the barren moor of my later life, I have sedulously avoided running my crazy head into what may be termed inconsequent distractions; and now, in spite of all my theoretical circumspection and security, I find myself over-head and ears, heart and soul, in love with you. I cannot for the life of me, help telling you so; but, as all considerate reason has not at times utterly abandoned me, I shall put myself into a strait-waistcoat and be chained to the bedpost.

"Perhaps, after having undergone such a compulsatory infliction, and the bereavement of at least half the blood in my veins, I may be restored to my more cool and sedate senses. I shall then turn Anchorite, and flee away to the desert. Adieu! I have yet sufficient command over my drooping faculties to restrain any tributary tears from falling over my farewell; you might doubt their reality; and we all know that they may be counterfeited upon paper, with a sponge and rose-water!

"*Addio, ben amata*—it was my intention to go to the sea-side for a day, and be dipped, as they treat unfortunates suffering under hydrophobia; but, without a miracle, I do not presume that I shall have regained force of resolution and intellect adequate to my attempting the voyage. And there, too, I should see you again, source and spirit of all my tribulations, and my cicatrizing wounds would bleed anew; still that would have been my sole object in going, to exist amphibiously, like an Undine, between raging billows and desolate rocks; and yet the shepherd in Virgil grew, at last, acquainted with Love, and found him a native of the rocks. But you would laugh clandestinely at me in your bustled sleeve; for there is nothing more ridiculous than a person in my desperate state; and I should only have to "bay the moon" with my solitary plaints, and exasperate you, and the winds and the waves, with my vain jeremiads. For the future, I shall haunt you with sentimental elegies upon mourning paper, with a death's head crucified upon bones, by way of an appropriate vignette.

"I think X—— beautiful, and I like her manner as much as her face. If you send me back the drawing, I shall suppose you are offended with me: keep it with you at Luc, that will be some consolation to me while I am at the St. Luke's of this place. What am I to do for a diurnal matinal correspondent and afternoon gossip, now that you are "over the hills and far away"? I am almost inclined to think that your sensibilities are as *marbrées* as your snowy complexion; still I shall ever be immutably yours in this world; and if our most devoted wishes and memories are allowed in the next, mine will still remain inviolable towards you.

GEORGE BRUMMELL."

Tuesday evening.

"May the recording angel, who registers above the amiable feelings and thoughts of mortals, preserve you for having written that last note to me! It has at once extricated me from the very abyss of gloomy and disconsolate reflections, and has restored me to peace and equanimity. After reading it, I sought another wander to the Cafarelli, and returned home to my solitary room at the hotel, contented with myself and all the world. I do not know myself again.

"I have this morning perambulated over this deserted town, acknowledged everyone whose physiognomy was familiar to me, *lancé* two bad jokes at His Excellency Monsieur le Baron de ——, in judgment of his new heathenish mouse-coloured pantaloons, and even disturbed my hat with my best strait-laced salutation to Madam d'A—— and her contemptible troop of monkeys in the shape of men. When I mentioned the Baron to you the other day, as having fallen into an inheritance, it was all mythological moonshine. Poor fellow! I believe he has nothing but his pantaloons and his misconceived *amour propre* to which he can look forward.

"Upon my knees I supplicate one of you to write to me, when you have not any more interesting objects to divert you, when the expanse of waters and the unfruitful waste of earth which surrounds you have wearied your unvaried prospect—pray write and tell me you think of me, be it so or not; "be for once forsworn", if you are thinking of anyone else; it will gratify me beyond all other sublunary blessings.

"Do not imagine that I am endeavouring to flatter you; I never did encourage such a subtle and degrading intention, and I never shall, but you write beautifully.

"I have sent you some books in continuation of *Les deux Fiancées*, which I have never read, by way of courier.

Ever yours,
G.B."

II

Another Christmas came. In his rooms at the Hotel d'Angleterre he was "as cold as a homeless dormouse". But to one of his lady friends he described a *bal masqué* at Madame de Rigny on New Year's Eve, at which he had galloped with the rest.

The *salon* of Madame de Rigny was somewhat mixed, for there one could see the ultra-Carlist, the *modéré* and the *juste milieu*, the Guizoistes, the Molistes and Thieristes; and the dancing was very prim and proper with *les jeunes demoiselles chaussées* in satin, and the gentlemen a little bit on the provincial side; but one could still jest and be thought the smartest man in Caen.

But towards the end of April he had another attack of paralysis: he was seized at the table-d'hôte, and he realized it because he felt his soup trickling down his chin. . . . He kept his presence of mind, and at once got up from the table, and quietly putting his napkin to his face, left the room with such perfect composure that no one imagined what had really happened. Before going to his room, that was reached by a secondary staircase on the other side of the courtyard, he went into the adjoining room, and looked in the looking-glass over the mantel. Alas, one glance was sufficient, for it showed that his mouth was drawn up to his ear; and he hastily retreated to his apartment.

He felt, indeed, desperate and worried. Would the disfigurement be permanent? He took off his coat, and let himself fall on the arm-chair. Till that day he had never owned to more than fifty years; indeed, only a little while ago he had asserted that a gentleman's age should be established at five-and-forty, unlike Louis Quatorze who had fixed it at seventy, *l'âge de tout le monde*!

A good physician came, humane and generous, who attended him without any fee. But he told him that it was necessary to shave a few hairs at the back of the head. These few mementoes of his former *chevelure* Brummell was most anxious to preserve, although they were usually concealed by his wig; and he asked the doctor, with a melancholy smile, whether it was absolutely necessary to lose them. The doctor replied that the blister could not be put on unless the precious hairs were removed. With becoming composure Brummell "handed" his head to the barber.

After this second attack he was under no illusions: "Do not ask me"—he wrote—"anything about my health; it makes me melancholy, and that *abaissement* sometimes makes me very childish. *Addio, cara amica.*"

"Miss Aimable" this year went early to Luc-sur-Mer. This thought saddened him a great deal. He, who had played at love all these years and kept so adroitly beyond the range of passion, now that he was old and ill and poor and no longer dazzling, was deeply in love with a girl young enough to be his daughter.

Before she left he gave her his album—the precious album that was the treasure-chest of his past. "You may, perhaps", he wrote to her, "find something in my old album to yawn over: what it contains was written in other and happier days, and most of them were given to me by the authors themselves, such as the Duchess of Devonshire, poor Byron and Sheridan." He revealed that the verses unsigned were the namby-pamby compositions of an unfortunate person who should be nameless, but whom she cut dead during the past several evenings. "It is but a poor old album indeed, and unworthy as a gift to you, but it has been for years the constant companion and friend of more solitary hours and has often solaced and diverted me through the many vicissitudes, errors and disappointments of my life." Alas, the Beau was getting sentimental.

Solitude was made dismal by poverty. He made friends with a little mouse that, one morning, came out of the wainscot of his so-called sitting-room at the Hotel d'Angleterre, and stood looking at him as if asking to share his breakfast. By dint of gentle training he taught the mouse to crawl up his leg on to the breakfast-table and to eat out of his hand.

The mouse made its regular appearance every morning, at the same hour. He became very much attached to it—like the prisoner's spider. One day the waiter threw a boot-jack at the little mouse and killed it. Brummell was much put out of spirits: he confided it to his dear friend with great embarrassment: "Madame de St. Ursain, were I to see a man and a dog drowning together in the same pond, and no one was looking on, I would prefer saving the dog!"

The hope of obtaining employment was but transient. His friends in London were bringing all the pressure they could upon Lord Palmerston, and one day, during summer, a message came from the Government that he should be prepared to leave. He replied to Earl Grenville, now Ambassador in Paris, enclosing a letter for Palmerston in which he hoped the direction would be toward Italy; and hopefully he mentioned it to "Miss Aimable": "Should this be awarded to me, I shall take up my wallet and staff and seek the auspicious haven of that country." But soon a reply came that there was at present no suitable vacancy

H

either in Italy or elsewhere. The fact was that the Foreign Office had been informed of the physical unfitness of Brummell at this time.

The disappointment was beyond words. The spasmodic attacks recurred again; and the anxiety of poverty increased. He sought relief in laudanum. Some days later he went to Luc-sur-Mer; would his chagrin be relieved in the long-desired company of "Miss Aimable"?

The journey was not a long one, for Luc-sur-Mer was only about nine miles from Caen. But it was a most unromantic spot. The accommodation for visitors was bad, and the sea-breeze was strongly impregnated with the smell of herrings. It was, as a seaside resort, much frequented by the fashionable people of the neighbouring towns: sometimes a few exclusives of the *haute société* of Paris came to Luc, afraid of the *bourgeois* crowd at Dieppe; there were, at Luc, the celebrated oysters from the Rochers de Cancale; but altogether it appeared to Brummell a vile caravanserai. Maybe his frame of mind contributed to make him find absurd the customs of the ladies, who, to be very careful of their complexions, took their parasols into the sea with them, and much noise and mock-modesty went on between the two groups of male and female bathers, separated by a wooden partition, and ablutions commenced to instrumental music. . . .

The real cause of irritation, however, was that "Miss Aimable" was not willing to accept the courtship of the aged Beau. And when a lonely man is in love, he may be inclined to overlook prudence.

On his return to Caen, there were new worries, ever increasing worries. The glorious release operated by Armstrong on his return from England was once again finished. His devoted friends had generously arranged with Armstrong to provide £120 a year to his general maintenance; but this again was little more than what his former consular salary had been after deducting what he had mortgaged to Leveux at Calais. Alas, even this small contribution of £120 a year was falling in arrears: were his friends in London deserting him? And Leveux of Calais was clamouring for the 15,000 francs still owing to him, to which there was a further 5,000 owing to the good Armstrong, and the bill for the *troisième* at the Hotel d'Angleterre was going up unpaid.

Worse than anything, unbearable even only to mention it, his wardrobe was now so threadbare that he had to write to Alvanley: "My old friend, King Allen had promised to send me some habiliments for my body, denuded like a new-born infant—and what a Beau I once was!" Indeed, indeed, it was heartbreaking to have to beg some clothes for he who was once Beau Brummell.

At the end of the year he suffered another attack of paralysis. It was less severe than the previous one, and he put up a brave front: "Miss Aimable" was now a debutante, and Brummell followed her from one *salon* to another, praising "her snowy complexion and beautiful eyebrows . . .". But in January 1835 a new storm of worries broke over him. Even François the valet wrote from Calais, to say that his old master's laundress was demanding money for the keep of a dog that Brummell had entrusted to her; and François wanted to know why Mr. Brummell had forgotten to secure for him the post he promised to recommend him; and Monsieur Leleux may have to give up *Le Pauvre Diable*. . . . Brummell answered, promising to send money for the keep of the dog Mouton "as soon as possible", and added that he would do "all in my power to obtain for you the work which you desire", and if M. Leleux had to part with his house "will you try to get hold for me of Loro the parrot . . .". Almost as an afterthought, he added in the letter: "I am told that M. Marshall thinks of leaving Calais, having been offered a better consulate. If you hear anything about that, let me know at once." "PS.—M. Dabert of Paris has written to me that he has a bill of 380 francs accepted by me, and due the 18th of this month, which will be presented to me here. Tell Valobra that I entrusted to him a little golden box with medallions in enamels, the value of which should have closed that claim, and that I shall not pay the bill in question before I know what has become of the said box, and another in *papier-mâché* which I gave him for a model." Poor Brummell!

In the spring "Miss Aimable" left Caen for England, to go there to complete her education. Brummell was desolate. "You are going away. It is a melancholy reflection for me that this is probably the last time I shall ever again write to you. Some day, perhaps ere long, you will read more of me, with the rest of the world who may give themselves the trouble. Enclosed, I send you letters for two of my oldest friends, high in their office at Court; you will be favourably received in the quarter to which they will present you. My nerves are too shattered, and my rheumatism too inveterate to enable me to call and take leave."

She wrote to him in April. "You do not know", he wrote back, "the good your letter has done me."

III

Ten days later, one fine day in May 1835, early in the morning, he was roughly awakened. He opened his eyes to look into the face of a jack-booted man—the figure of Justice. The *huissier* produced a writ of arrest, at the suit of M. Leveux of Calais, for fifteen thousand francs, and intimated that unless he could pay the amount forthwith he must go to prison. Brummell, who did not clearly understand, and felt ill at ease without his wig, requested that they would allow him to dress; but the unpleasant-looking man ordered him to put on his clothes without more ado and follow him immediately. At this, Brummell broke down. He prayed, he groaned, lamented and finally gave way to the most trivial despair.

He had to get out of bed and slip on his clothes before the intruders. For the first time in his life, he was under the necessity of dressing in a hurry.

In the meantime his landlady, Madame Fichet, had sent a servant to several of Brummell's friends to acquaint them of his arrest; but the sum was too large for any kind of intervention. Of this Brummell himself was well aware; and he sent for a coach to take him to prison—a coach which he had not the money to pay for. He also entreated Madame Fichet to take care of all his papers: "They are the only things I possess to which I attach particular value; they are of no use to anyone else, *mais pour moi, Madame Fichet, ils sont un vrai trésor*; when I am gone, pray collect them and lock them up with your own hands." A waiter came to announce that the *fiacre* was ready. Two *gendarmes* and the *huissier* got in the coach with their prisoner, and they moved to their sad destination.

On his arrival at the gaol he was locked up in a cell with common prisoners. The floor was of stone, and the furniture consisted only of the three truckle-beds of his companions; there were no chairs, but one was brought in for his use.

The next day a friend came to condole and brought messages from the ladies. Brummell managed to send a note to a friend: it was hastily written in pencil and scarcely legible.

In Prison, 5th May 1835.

"I still breathe, though I am not of the living—the state of utter abstraction in which I have been during the last thirty hours yet clouds my every sense. I have just received your note—may heaven bless you all for your good devotedness in remembering me at such a moment.

"I have been the victim of a villain, who has closed upon me, without giving me the remotest intimation of his designs. I am perfectly innocent of anything bearing the least dishonourable construction in this *malheureuse affaire*; and if I was not deserving of the interest you express towards me, I would not demand it.

"I will write to you when I can. Ever most sincerely yours.

G.B."

The day after his arrest, his friends, both English and French, exerted themselves to obtain for him the indulgence of a private room; but the gaol was very full. One of the judges, however, permitted Brummell to share, during the day, the apartment of a Monsieur Godefroi, a journalist who, as *gérant responsable* for a legitimist paper called *L'Ami de la Verité*, was confined to prison for a political offence. At night Brummell had to sleep in a narrow passage communicating with another part of the prison— a corridor barely wider than his bed, but it was a paradise compared with the common room. The view from the window of this corridor was not a very cheering one; through the bars on the left Brummell could see the courtyard of the women prisoners, whose hands were generally busy at their distaffs, while their lips emitted raucous and vulgar words. In front was the yard and small garden of *La Pistole*, and farther to the right was the yard called *La Paille*, from the material on which the prisoners slept, in contradistinction to the wool-beds of the former. Beyond this was the outer wall of the prison, the roofs of the houses in the Quartier St. Martin, and the tops of a few lime trees. But the view of the green trees was small compensation, and in the daytime Brummell descended the forty steps to the cell of M. Godefroi, which was considered the best in the prison: one could contemplate, down below, the fellows condemned to the galleys.

His letters tell us that he suffered from want of food, but even more from want of soap.

In Prison, May 11.

"The kindness of every human being within the sphere of my acquaintance in this town has by degrees restored me to equanimity. How shall I be able to repay you for this benevolence? Devoutly I thank you for *The Student*; it will be an early resource to me. I am, I believe, this evening to be transferred from my present den of thieves to the towers of Matilda, and to the sainted arms of *les soeurs de Charité*. There I shall again breathe fresh air, and be comparatively in peace. I cannot describe to you what I have suffered here.

"H——, in the frequent moments I have seen him since his return, has felt and acted towards me with the affection of a brother. I cannot today trust myself further in writing to you; remembrance of you and those who belong to you will crowd upon my thoughts, and I might relapse into my recent imbecilities by the endeavour. Adieu! Persevere in all your excelling goodness towards me. It may please Providence to guide the hearts of those who once better knew me to imitate your kindness.

Ever sincerely yours,

G.B.

"PS. You will perceive the extremities to which I am reduced—I am about to seal to you with a wafer! Do not even whisper this indecorum, for perhaps I may again frequent the world."

In Prison, Saturday.

"Dear Armstrong,

"Henri de St. Marie told me yesterday you had sent me a bottle of *Esprit de Savon*—I have never received it. If it had been left to Bassy, the chemist, to send, of course I shall never see it; should it have been remitted for conveyance to the hotel, equal negligence will attend its destiny. In spite of all my friends have said to them in expostulation of the shameful pitifulness of the morsel they send to me by way of dinner, they get daily more meagre and miserable, and it is really not sufficient for the poor cat that keeps me company, neither does it arrive before half-past six, *malgré* your orders to them. I cannot help telling you what was the banquet yesterday dispatched to me: one solitary chop, about the size of an *écu*, enveloped in a quire of greasy paper, and the skeleton of a pigeon, a bird I could never fancy. I must not omit to mention the accompaniment of half a dozen potatoes. Such was the meal of yesterday evening, after a fast of

232

twelve hours. It is not, I am certain, the fault of the son, but the *ladrerie* of the *père et mère*, with which I have been so long acquainted. If they transmit me nothing more solid and bountiful this evening, I shall be reduced to borrow a *tranche* of the *bouilli* from which the *soupe maigre* of my neighbours the brigands is extracted. I have not seen a soul today. I have no news, and I am in the very slough of despondency.

Yours,

G.B."

In Prison, Monday.

"My dear Armstrong,

"Many thanks for your unremitting kindness, in improving the quality of my humble repast. To your good offices, I had yesterday the satisfaction of being indebted for a sufficient though homely dinner.

"I have sent to you two serviettes, which I had neglected, belonging to the Hotel d'Angleterre; they are the last remaining in my possession from that quarter. You will oblige me by sending to me, today, three towels for my *toilette*; and the same number every six days, for I cannot procure even a clout to rub myself down in this nauseous place. You will not, I am sure, forget either that every three days it is incumbent on me to pay for the necessities of breakfast, eau-de-vie, candles, etc.—while you are here or during your absence.

"I will beg you carefully to take charge of everything I left behind me at the hotel, particularly two boxes; the one mahogany with brass ribs, and G.B. on a plate at the top—the other with a glass top, covering worked birds drinking out of a vase; it was the labour and gift of the Duchess of York, and I have a reverence for it—the latter has a leather case, which is either in the cupboard or the *armoire* out of the sitting-room, or in the other recess where you will find my trunks, etc., etc. Pray send me what remains in the drawers of the bedroom—there are some waistcoats, drawers, pantaloons, etc., and in the upper *tiroir*, sundry trifling things which I forgot, but which I may have occasion for. The clock, vases, brown candlesticks, and in short everything in the room is my own, not omitting the old green velvet arm-chair. There is one insignificant article which I also wish you would transmit to me: it is under the small commode in the sitting-room, with a white marble slab on the top (which also belongs to me), and of which I am every evening in want, a bootjack that shuts up. Let the large basin and water-jug be taken care of.

"This is all that I can recollect—perhaps there may be other trifles in the *armoire*, adjoining the sitting-room, which at the instant escape my memory; let them be preserved.

"Enclosed, I deliver to you a list of every debt which I owe in this country of France; you will have the goodness to add your own just and excellent claims upon me, and those due to the hotel—those in the list to whose names I have attached a cross. I am ignorant of the precise amount of their remaining claims upon me; you can easily ascertain them. Beyond these, so help me Heaven, I have not an existing debt, either in my handwriting, or by oral promise, in this country. Young B—— is waiting below to carry my letter; therefore, I can only add, my dear Armstrong, how very sincerely,

I am, yours,

G.B."

The indispensables of his toilet arrived at the prison, one by one, sent by Armstrong, by Henri de St. Marie and by several of the adoring ladies.

An intelligent man can manage even in prison; and in a twinkle of an eye Brummell had hired one of the other prisoners, a Paul Lapine, a former drummer of the army, as his valet. The leader-writer Godefroi became day after day accustomed to the most extraordinary *toilette* anyone could ever imagine within the cell of a gaol. "*Il consacrait,*" Godefroi used to tell in years after, "*trois heures à sa toilette.*" Each detail was executed with extreme attention. He actually washed and shaved every day; each day he made a complete ablution of each part of his body, using the large basin of an old lavabo that had joined him in prison, together with the dressing-case which was full of bottles of oils and of cosmetics. For this operation of daily cleanliness, unheard of in the history of prison-life, he used each day from twelve to fifteen litres of water and two litres of milk expressly brought to him each morning by an anonymous donor. His valet Lapine he had re-named Lafleur, and he, an old officer, had been quick enough to size-up the drummer Lapine as an excellent batman. The fun was that Lafleur was immensely proud to valet his new master; he never regretted the climbing of steps he had to make to carry upstairs all the water. The only thing that worried him was the waste of those two litres of milk which could have been so easily and profitably converted in a couple of glasses of eau-de-vie!

Soon Brummell overcame the problem of food. The adoring ladies of Calais sent him in "their benefaction *en forme de gateaux*": they thought of him not as a prisoner but as an invalid, and they sent him hampers of wine and jellies and *pâtés*. He replied with witty and cheerful notes, asking for some tit-bits also for his companion Minette, "*la chatte noire*, who is in the straw at my feet, having produced three hungry kittens—her delicate state disdains the unleavened bread of the prison".

His friends also thought of the dreariness of the evening, and in the basket which carried the provisions were also a few volumes of light reading; they were always thankfully received: "If *The Student* had not belonged to you, I should not have been able to wade through ten of its pages; and I can only wonder that the author of *Eugene Aram* and *Pompei* should have buried his brains in such a production. I cannot tell you how much it gratifies me to know that your *domestique* brings my daily bread from the hotel: these trifling circumstances do one worlds of good at the moment. Good-bye for the evening. My friend Godefroi, the editor, from whose table I address you, is looking with anxiety at the ink, to continue paragraphs that will probably prolong his detention here ten years longer. He is really a good-hearted man, and does everything *à me distraire*. Say everything that is gracious for me to . . .

"Ever sincerely yours,
"G.B."

One day it happened to be a French translation of Byron's *Life*, and he turned the pages over with rapidity, reading aloud, and with an air of great satisfaction and apparent pride: "*Oui*," he said to Godefroi, "*ce poète, ce grand homme, fut mon ami.*" It was the only time that his fellow-prisoner ever heard him allude to his former position.

Each day at two o'clock he descended to the debtor's courtyard for his exercise: after spending three hours at his *toilette*, well-groomed, with shining boots, with his neck-cloth as white and well tied, his hat smoothed to a hair, as perfect as if he had been going to pay a visit to one of his ladies. In this courtyard, separated from that of thieves and other criminals by a thin partition, between

the hours of two and four he received his numerous visitors
—and his prison levees were well attended and merry
enough. But if anyone offered to condole for the tardiness
of his release, his gaiety soon evaporated.

One day a rich Carlist of Caen was brought in, Baron
de Bresmenil, to serve a sentence of five days for "treason",
as driving in his carriage he had responded to the cries of
supporters of Louis Philippe with cries of "Vive Henri
Cinq!" The Baron decided to celebrate his incarceration
with a grand dinner from Longuet's, and allowed Brummell to select his favourite dishes. The chief guest from
outside was another friend of Brummell's, the Comte de
Roncherolles, who brought a bottle of brandy d'Andaye,
of which Brummell was very fond. When the dinner was
over, and Brummell's features reflected the pleasure of
the *hors-d'œuvres* and the entrée, of the mushroom and the
truffle, of the *homards* and the *fruits glacés*, of the Chamber-
tin and the Lafitte, he rose above his misfortunes, and
related with much humour anecdotes of his early life.
The Comte de Roncherolles announced his bottle of old
eau-de-vie d'Andaye, and Brummell turned to one of the
three young thieves who had waited at dinner: "Fetch
the bottle, fetch the bottle: my dear Roncherolles, no
cognac I ever tasted can be compared to your d'Andaye!"

But the petty larcenist who left the room for the brandy,
did not return: another was sent to hasten him, and the
third, but none came back: till the attendants returned
with the message that the brandy of Monsieur le Comte
had disappeared! The Baron, who was as tall and brawny
as a Hercules, threatened to throw the three footmen out
of the window, forgetting that his present windows were
well furnished with bars. In the midst of the fray Brummell
rose from his chair, and spreading his arms towards the
three delinquents, he shrieked out: "*Malheureux! On ne*

vous a que trop bien traités. Scelerats, rendez-moi mon pousse-café!'' This energetic address became more pathetic when one of the party returned with the information that not the three thieves but the turnkey, Brillant, to whose special care the cognac had been confided, had drained it to the last drop, and was lying insensible, snoring in a corner!

In the middle of July things began to look brighter. Armstrong had undertaken yet another, and this time most urgent, journey to London. It was a difficult task, for some of the old friends, who had assisted Brummell so many times, were not inclined to be greatly impressed by his dire plight. But Armstrong, unembarrassed by feelings of delicacy, undertook the collection of donations as a man of business, and he found two splendid supporters in the Duke of Beaufort and that staunchest of Brummell's friends, Lord Alvanley. Their influence induced many other friends to subscribe to a fund for Brummell's release from prison. One of the donors was King William IV, who personally knew very little of Brummell, but subscribed one hundred pounds when Brummell's deplorable condition was brought to his notice. This generous act of the King influenced Lord Palmerston who added £200 from the Treasury. Armstrong then collected £250 more, in gifts of £25 each from the Duke of Devonshire, Lord Sefton, General Upton, General Grosvenor, Colonel Howard, Charles Greville, and many others. The Duke of Beaufort, Alvanley, Sefton and Greville gave, furthermore, assurance to provide annually for poor Brummell.

On the morning of the 21st of July, an attorney by the name of M. Youf came to the prison, and notified to Brummell that his debt to M. Leveux had been paid, and that he was at liberty to leave the prison when he pleased.

To the astonishment of everyone, Brummell received the information without manifesting the slightest surprise or joy. At five o'clock in the afternoon, after an imprisonment of two months and seventeen days, he left the gaol with an air of insouciance, and returned to the Hotel d'Angleterre, and went up to his rooms as if returning from a visit to the seaside.

That same evening he presented himself at a large soirée at the General's. He advanced towards the centre of the room, and as the company, who had not heard of his release, could not suppress their surprise, he bowed his thanks right and left: "Gentlemen, I am extremely grateful for your kindness, and charmed to be once again with you; I can assure you that it is today the happiest day of my life for I have just come out of prison," and here he paused, and then gravely added: "and I have eaten some excellent salmon."

IV

But it was all a make-believe. He deluded himself that it was a great thing to be free again, "to go about" in the world. Back at the *troisième* at the Hotel d'Angleterre he had looked at his things, his few miserable possessions, that were all that was left of his former grandeur. His clock, his vases, his candlesticks, the brass-ribbed mahogany box with "G.B." inlaid on top, and the box with the birds under glass that had been worked for him by the Duchess of York, and his precious toilet things, and most of all his green velvet arm-chair. And to open his trunks, and look at his wardrobe—or what was left of it.

And now that Armstrong had paid all the debts, it seemed almost as if life could start afresh. Indeed, it was a pleasure to send some partridges to the good Godefroi who was still in prison : "*Grondez, mon cher Monsier Godefroi, le perfide chef de cuisine et non pas ma fidèle memoire*, for having so long delayed the offer of a little covey of patridges, nested in their wall of crust. . . . Be good enough to address my friendly regards to the gallant Father Bassy, and let him share at least a leg. . . . I beg to prostrate myself and my gentle souvenirs to the velvet pads of Mademoiselle Minette, and remember me to the worthy Lavigne and his twin Baptiste. You will be delighted to hear that we have recently seen perched upon the coach, en route to Honfleur, our ci-devant valet Lafleur, as gay as the coach that was carrying him, clasping in his Achillean arms the nice waist of a captured princess with a hat crowned with three feathers, red like her blooming cheeks!"

But, as usual, he was too neglectful, too impertinent with some of the people of Caen. To some who had been kind to him during his imprisonment he was profuse with thanks; others he neglected altogether: he appeared to think that by assuming an air of flippant indifference he could throw a veil over the events of the last three months. One of these acquaintances was one of the Judges, who, in his official capacity, had been of great service to him. This Judge, a man of quick repartee, shared the table d'hôte at the Hotel d'Angleterre, and had the weakness to consider himself an expert on horsemanship and on dress, both of which, with him, were execrably bad: he used to wear a white macintosh that was so stiff that when in the saddle it made him rattle like an armadillo out of repair. But Brummell had a far stronger motive for disliking him: the Judge actually kept a toothpick, a permanent pinchback toothpick, which, from its antique appearance, had probably belonged to his great-grandfather, and had therefore been used to pick the teeth of four generations, a disgusting idea. Brummell used to say: "Corpo di Bacco, a most horrible practice!" It happened that about a fortnight after he had regained his liberty, he met the learned Judge in the street, and though he had not cared to call upon him and express his thanks, he greeted him lightly: "Ah, mon cher Aréopagite, I am so sorry not to have paid you my little visit; but the fact is that my visiting-cards which are always made in London, have not yet arrived." "Really!" answered the vexed Judge with a very stiff bow in his white macintosh. "Do not trouble at all, Monsieur Brummell; if you had made me that honour, I could not have returned it for you, for at the moment I too am without cards, and mine are always made in China!"

But impertinence and *sans souci*, it was all a make-believe. A lady said: "I regret having lost several letters and some poetry he has sent to me; they were full of the sadness he felt in his solitude, that was pushing him to recall the brilliant past and the present so sad, and the future so frightening to think of. . . . Yet he affected to challenge Fortune and to laugh at her blows."

Yes, the people of Caen still looked at him when he took a walk; and rich travellers at the hotel made advances with a glass of champagne so as to hear him talk and recount his personal history: but where was his exclusiveness, that was so formidable in the London days?

But "Miss Aimable" returned from England a young woman of nineteen, not quite so yielding to the doubtful fascination of a man who was no longer Beau Brummell, and nearly forty years her senior. Short of his album, which he had already given her, he searched his papers for something that might attract her; he drew sketches of her: "*Daignez agréer l'offrande d'un esquisse pour votre* album. I am discontented with it; it is too deeply shaded, and that fault has been unavoidable from the *maudit papier qui buvait* whenever my contending *crayon* came in contact (pretty alliteration) with its spongy surface. Receive it as it is; the only merit to which it may pretend is, its being original: as you said of some of my other productions, I never copied anything or anybody. Deny me not your thanks for the drawing: and if you are the same amiable creature that you used to be in our earlier acquaintance, tell me that I may still cherish the faith of existing *sempre* in your continued friendship." But did she tell him? Ah, the poor old Beau, still trying to be witty with the girl of nineteen: "I am too much saddened by the shadows of Vallombrosa, at Madame de Seran's last night, to hold my head up if I saw you. I shall take to rouge if this goes on. . . ."

Take to rouge—yes, to rouge his very heart, his very
soul, walking blindly on, with eyes closed to the tragedy
that is closing in. The ladies are beseeching him to give
them souvenirs, some relics of his old days in England.
What! Do they consider him already a corpse? But he
walked on and on, the same *soirées*, and the same whist
parties, the same habits as before, two hours in his tub,
two hours before the looking-glass; he read, he drew, he
wrote notes to his lady acquaintances, dined, "drank tea"
with a friend, and gave some relics to this or that privileged lady, the bits that had been presented to him "by
his titled and fashionable friends of Langsyne. . . ."
"Upon ransacking other debris of former times, I cannot
find any note-keepers in better preservation than the two
wrecks you now receive. Their only recommendation
may be that the green one was worked by Lady Sarah
Saville; the other, of the dove tint, like her eyes, was the
travail of Lady Foley; both of them at that halcyon
period, blooming in surpassing beauty!"

Yes, it was all a make-believe. For his finances were in
a pitiful state. If Brummell had no more debts—comparatively speaking—he neither had any more income.
The coming out of prison had given him, for a short
while, a new prestige, almost a credit, "a man who had
paid his debts". But his income was what it was, the
meagre £120 a year, which had been promised by his
friends in London, and half of which Armstrong had to
pay to Madame Fichet for his board and lodgings at the
Hotel d'Angleterre, and the rest was for wine, fire, washing and clothes, and if anything remained out of the £60
it could be used for the incidental expenses which his
peculiar habits made endless. This income of £120 was
£40 more than Brummell technically had during his
consulship after mortgaging four-fifths of his salary to

the banker Leveux; but it still was a very small income.

Nor could Brummell, not even after his experience of prison, be converted to the idea of thrift. He could do without many things, but he could not do without the multitude of etceteras which were the necessity of his very existence: a man of Brummell's cast could do without necessities but not without the luxuries.

Towards the end of the year things were getting again in a muddle. The wise and watchful Armstrong brought him to give up three changes of shirts and cravats a day, and be quite content with one. But Brummell could not in his heart resign himself to renounce his primrose gloves, his eau-de-Cologne, the oil for his wig, and most of all his patent blacking for his boots. This last was the subject of a correspondence with Armstrong:

November, 1836

"My dear Armstrong,

"Mulet, the bootmaker, has this instant been with me, in an insolent manner, and says that as you have refused positively to pay his account, or the principal part of it, for *vernis*, he shall proceed against me for the amount of this debt, unless it is settled the present day. Send me the money on my account. I have not four francs in my possession, and it will utterly destroy me to see a bailiff enter my room, or assault me in the street.

"I will enter into any promise with you upon the subject of this d——d polish that you demand, if you will instantly enable me to pay this scoundrel.

Most truly yours,

G.B."

This *vernis de Guiton* he used to order expressly from Paris and it cost five francs a bottle. "Dear Armstrong," he wrote again a month later. "Do not be any more out of temper with me. I do not deserve it from you; I have never trespassed upon the rules of economy which you dictated to me, excepting in one instance, *and that has been for that d——d execrable blacking. I have now relinquished it for ever!*" And the pitiful letter, with the avowal that brought tears to his eyes—his blacking!—was ending with a more pitiful confession: "I am not ashamed to tell you candidly that I have not two *sous* remaining of the twenty francs you had the goodness to send me."

He tried a lottery, without any luck. The lottery office lodged a claim in December. "Dear Armstrong, You have hurt me more than I can express by your note to me this morning. I will never again commit such an extravagant and senseless error. But do not allow the precipitate anger of the moment to damp and destroy your friendly efforts to save me. I will endeavour to write, the instant I am restored to calmness, to the Duke of Devonshire. It would afflict me to suppose that my immediate unfortunate affairs interfered with your better interests in other quarters." This was a reference to Armstrong's desire to be appointed Vice-Consul in Caen.

At last, Armstrong put his foot down: such cleanliness as a shirt and neckcloth every day was a great extravagance. What a sadness not to be any more a paragon of cleanliness! And then the last blow came, though Armstrong did not have the heart to inflict it himself, and got a lady to do the work: his white cravat had to go. The lady told him, in a jocular manner, that his looks, as a mature man, would be improved by a black cravat. Brummell went immediately to his comptroller, and having obtained permission to purchase one, to the amazement of his friends, he appeared the next morning in the Rue St. Jean in what had all his life been his particular aversion—a black silk neckerchief!

V

Was it the finger of Fate? The black cravat was the signal of the end, his own mourning of his now departed elegance. His self-respect vanished with the black cravat.

Now he would dine with anyone who would pay the bill. His memory gave way, he would repeat the same story over and over again. He became careless in his manners; indeed he became filthy—so filthy that people in the hotel objected to his presence in the dining-room. His white foamy cravat, his emblem to which he had clung with affection all his life, was now gone, and Brummell the Beau died that day—snowy cambric gently starched had become to him matters of history. The decayed and diminished state of his wardrobe, that he had now no prospect of replenishing, was an additional reason for such a dereliction of all his former principles.

He was in need of a dressing-gown; instead of a shawl one that he had applied for, suitable for winter wear, Armstrong sent him a cotton one. When Brummell unfolded the garment he was so enraged that he threw it out of the window; the unlucky dressing-gown landed upon the diligence of Bayeux. And yet, a few weeks later he must write to Armstrong: "I have not a single shirt that will hang to my back, nor are my socks and drawers in a better state!"

The St. Ursains leave Caen for good. His oldest and dearest friends. He took leave by letter; he could not stand to appear in such a deplorable state, and in such agony of mind, before the "Miss Aimable" who had won the love of his old age.

"It disappointed me much not to shake hands with you *en adieux* yesterday. It was perhaps the last occasion I shall find in the world to express my devoted gratitude to you and yours, for all your kindness towards me: may we meet as good friends in the next! Pray, while you enact the chaperon with all commendable discretion, do not forget the spirit of indulgence for youthful feeling that pervades the lines in my old album, "Oh let the young enthusiast stray." Tell her also, for it is the simple unassuming truth, that wherever I may hereafter sojourn, far away, she will never, for an hour, be forgotten by me. Adieu! and may you all be happy! God bless you.

Ever sincerely yours,
GEORGE BRUMMELL."

And now, what mattered?

One day, Tom Moore, the poet and songster, came to see him in Caen. Tom Moore! Oh, memories of London, of Byron, of Georgiana Duchess of Devonshire! Tom Moore, who had been one of the three poet-members of Watier's. It was like a resurrection from the grave. But it was too late. Were there some in London who remembered his sartorial tyranny? And his exquisite elegance of manners and of wit? Moore was shaken with pity. To the friends in London he reported: "The poor Beau's head is gone, and his whole looks so changed that I should never have recognized him."

Now he did not care any longer to go about in tatters: he threw his old green coat with the worn-out fur collar over his holes. Only his tailor at Caen felt sorry for him: "*J'ai honte de voir un homme si célèbre et si distingué, et avec une place dans l'histoire, dans un état si malheureux.*" Yes, yes, a man so famous and so distinguished, and with a place in history, in such a disgraceful condition! And the tailor, the plain provincial tailor, had pity on the decayed Beau, and not being able to afford to give him some new clothes, he kept him in such repair as was still possible.

He became a glutton, as greedy of sweet things as a child. He was fond of *biscuits de Rheims*, he was greedy for a little glass of Curaçao. Unable to pay for them, he would go to the confectionery shop of Monsieur Magdalaine off the Place Royale and beg to have it on his account. He used to drink a cup of coffee, eat two of his biscuits which were always favoured by a glass of Curaçao, and paid for them with a bow. When the shop showed reluctance he began to sell his trinkets and the things that even in this poverty he considered part of himself; and now he pawned them for a few *sous*. And to procure some perfumed oil for his wig he disposed of a handsome repeater to an Englishman of the name of Pitt, a tulle manufacturer of Caen; it had originally cost eighty guineas and now was sold for a very small sum; no one knew who negotiated the sale, for the man Pitt was not in the circle of Brummell. So went the porcelain vases, another watch, the seals, and a chain, and even his last silver snuff-box was pledged to Monsieur Magdelaine for more *biscuits de Rheims*. But he never sold a single thing to his equals: a friend, one day, offered him a sum for his ormolu greyhound which he kept upon the mantelshelf. Brummell refused it: "If you are interested in it, pray accept it, but I won't sell it."

Some people still received him—his faithful and loyal hostesses; but he was now such a driveller and he fell asleep by the fireplace. Yet, in all his rags, he would still walk on his tip-toes from cobble to cobble, making sure the rain did not splash the boots that were no longer shining with Guiton's polish. One night he slipped and fell, and the urchins laughed and shrieked after him: "There goes *Monsieur Brummell le Dandy*!"

Now the voice went round the drawing-rooms that his mind was going—he was having delusions; the hotel's valet had said it. The "old man"—the valet had said—was now quite mad; he was holding receptions with ghosts? Receptions? With the ghosts? The hostesses of Caen shuddered and sighed.

One cold and gloomy winter afternoon a foreign lady arrived at the Hotel d'Angleterre, without equipage, servant or luggage. The stranger was of a certain age and plainly dressed, but, to the hostler's eye, unmistakably a great lady. She requested to be given a private room, and asked the landlord: "Is Mr. Brummell still living in this hotel? I am most anxious to see him. Can you put me in the way of doing so, without the chance of his seeing me?" "At five o'clock, Madame, he usually opens his door: you will be quite able to see him from the door of the opposite room on the same landing."

Who was this lady? Was she Lady Jersey, the former patroness of Almack's, who had imposed upon herself this pilgrimage, not to a shrine but to a living grave? At five o'clock she stood in the dark frame of her door and put a hand to her mouth to stifle a cry. In the shabby, almost bare room across the landing, a whist table was laid, and two *bougies* were lit, with cheap tallow. The valet stood at the door, announcing the ghosts: "Lady Conyngham! Lord Yarmouth! Her Grace Georgiana Duchess of Devonshire!" And the Beau, in his tattered suit, rose from his chair and advanced towards the door, and greeted the cold air from the staircase, and bowed low and gracefully to the ghosts. "Ah, my dear Duchess, how rejoiced I am to see you! Pray bury yourself in this arm-chair: do you know, it was a gift from the Duchess of York? . . ."

The ghosts, the ghosts! The mysterious lady ran down the stairs, pulling down her veil to hide her tears. She left a gold *louis* on the counter, and mounting in her chaise she departed at once, and was gone with the ghosts upstairs.

EPILOGUE

Now his beard was unshaved and his mind was utterly gone. And illness made him unclean. The Beau was lost to the world.

One morning, in May 1839, his landlord, Fichet, ordered a carriage to be drawn nearest to the secondary staircase that led to the shabby apartment on the *troisième*. He went upstairs with Mr. Armstrong, and they found Brummell in his arm-chair by the fire, the chair which had been given to him by the Duchess of York; sitting there with his wig upon his knees, and dipping his brush into an old pewter shaving-box which stood on the table, lathering the wig prior to shaving it. "*Bonjour*, M. Brummell, would you like to come for a little drive?" "*Laissez-moi tranquille*," and he went on with his lathering. They coaxed him. They took him away forcibly. He cried: "Am I going back to prison? Oh no, Armstrong, not that!"

No, it was not prison; it was the Bon Sauveur, a pious institution for the mentally deranged. A nun met them, and Brummell mistook her for Auguste, Armstrong's servant. The nun smiled, while Brummell, totally unconscious of its absurdity, shyly added: "*Ah, vous êtes mariée! Eh bien, je vous félicite, car. . . .*" And he added: "*Vous êtes bien une jolie femme.*"

They took him to his new room, with a blazing fire and an arm-chair in front of it; it was the room that had formerly been occupied by Bourrienne, Napoleon's A.D.C., who, like Brummell, had seen the ups and downs of glory in life.

251

And there, in the peace of the Bon Sauveur, Brummell spent his last few months. On the evening of his death, about an hour before he expired, the debility having become extreme, he assumed an appearance of intense anxiety and fear, and his eyes fixed upon the Institution Priest with an expression of entreaty, raising his hands, as he lay in the bed, as though imploring assistance, but saying nothing. Then he was quiet, and died quietly. It was a quarter past nine in the evening of the 30th of March 1840.

He was buried in the dreary Protestant cemetery of Caen, a wilderness of weeds and fennel, with a plain slab of black marble erected by his brother and sister.

Such is the story of George Brummell. He had not been rich, he had not been noble, yet his memory and his name live for ever. For he was King "by the grace of Grace".

Weybridge, 1957

BIBLIOGRAPHY

ASHTON, JOHN: *Old Times*. A Picture of Social Life at the End
of the Eighteenth Century.
  Social England Under the Regency.
BARBEY D'AUREVILLY, J. A.: *Du Dandisme et de George Brum-
mell.*
BOUTET DE MONVEL, R.: *Beau Brummell and His Times.*
BOULANGER, JACQUES: *Les Dandys.*
BERESFORD, CHANCELLOR: *Life in the Regency and Early Vic-
torian Times.*
BERKELEY, GRANTLEY: *Life and Recollections.*
BOURKE, HON. A. B.: *History of White's.*
BULWER-LYTTON, E. G.: *Pelham or the Adventures of a Gentle-
man.*
CONNELLY, W.: *The Reign of Beau Brummell.*
CORRY, JOHN: *Satirical View of London Men and Manners.*
FILON, AUGUSTINE P. M.: *La Caricature en Angleterre.*
FORGUES, E. D.: *Originaux et Beaux Esprits de l'Angleterre Con-
temporaine.*
GRANVILLE, LADY HARRIET: *Letters (1810–45).*
HUISH, ROBERT: *Memoirs of George IV.*
GRONOW, CAPT. R. H.: *Reminiscences.*
  Recollections and Anecdotes.
JESSE, CAPTAIN: *The Life of Beau Brummell.*
CAMPBELL, K.: *Beau Brummell.*
LISTER, T. H.: *Granby.*
MELVILLE, L.: *Beau Brummell: His Life and Letters.*
QUENNELL, P.: *Byron: The Years of Fame.*
RAIKES, T.: *Journals.*
WHEATLEY, H. B.: *Round About Piccadilly and Pall Mall.*
WILSON, HARRIETTE: *Memoirs.*
WRAXALL, SIR N. W.: *Historical Memoirs of My Own Time.*
WOOLF, V.: *Beau Brummell.*

INDEX